Graphic design: Zapp
Chef/stylist: Josée Robitaille
Photography: Nathalie Dumouchel
Typesetting: Typotech Inc.

Additional recipes: Arlene Gryfe
Institut de tourisme et d'hôtellerie du Québec

Tableware/props courtesy of: Pier 1 Imports
Ramacieri Design Inc.
Stokes

Copyright © 1997 Tormont Publications Inc.
338 Saint Antoine Street East
Montreal, Canada H2Y 1A3
Tel: (514) 954-1441
Fax: (514) 954-5086

ISBN 2-7641-0485-5
Printed in the U.S.A.

CONTENTS

INTRODUCTION

What a pleasure it is to bite into a delicious cookie, straight from the oven!

There's something truly magical about homemade cookies: they warm the heart, light up the face, please the palate and even, at times, bring comfort. Generations have treated themselves to cookies at snack time, coffee breaks, tea-time, on picnics, for dessert, as midnight snacks...and whenever else they can get the chance.

In each chapter you will find a different variety of cookie: refrigerator cookies, drop cookies, cutout cookies, shaped cookies, chocolate cookies, filled and garnished cookies, and holiday cookies, not to mention cookies from around the world. There is also a chapter devoted to bars and squares, and another to muffins. And with over 250 superb color photos and step-by-step techniques to guide you, baking a batch any time couldn't be easier.

From partytime and snacking cookies which are a hit with children, to the more elegant holiday and international specialties; from nutritious bars prepared in a jiffy, to hearty and savory muffins, *The Ultimate Cookie Book* offers recipes for all tastes and occasions.

Whichever recipe you're following, certain basic cooking rules should be followed in order to achieve the best results. Here are some tips that will make it easy, and ensure you have delicious cookies, squares and muffins each and every time.

- Measure the ingredients carefully, according to the quantities given in the recipe. Prepare them in advance and keep butter at room temperature, ready for use.

- Unless otherwise stated, prepare the dough with an electric mixer, but do not overmix it or the cookies will be hard. Cookies mixed by hand are generally more compact and dense.

- Sift the dry ingredients together first and set them aside. Combine the shortening, oil, butter or margarine with the sugar and the eggs, then mix in the dry ingredients.

- Preheat the oven and prepare the cookie sheets ahead of time. Preferably, use non-stick cookie sheets that are easy to clean and ensure even baking. Regular cookie sheets must be greased and floured, or greased and lined with parchment paper or ovenproof waxed paper.

- In a given recipe, make cookies the same size and the same thickness to ensure even baking.

- For drop cookies and shaped cookies, be sure to leave enough space between cookies to allow room for them to spread out on the cookie sheet during baking.

- For cutout cookies, refrigerate the dough 1 to 2 hours before rolling it out and cutting into cookies. To roll out the dough, use a rolling pin and lightly flour your work surface; if you flour it too much, the dough will absorb the excess flour and the cookies will be dry. The thinner the dough, the crisper the cookies.

- To check cookies for doneness in the oven, press down lightly in the middle. If they bounce back, they are done. In general, they are cooked when they turn golden or the edges begin to brown. When you take them out of the oven, remove the cookies immediately from the cookie sheet in order to stop the cooking process.

○ Place the cookies on a wire rack to allow them to cool evenly.

○ Keep cookies in an airtight container so that they stay crisp. Store soft cookies in an airtight container with a slice of apple wrapped loosely in waxed paper.

○ To melt chocolate, chop it coarsely and place it in a clean, dry, stainless steel bowl. Place the bowl above a saucepan half-full of simmering water. The bottom of the bowl should not touch the water. Let the chocolate melt slowly.

These tips are in addition to the clear and precise instructions found throughout the book. In most cases, they will make it so easy that shaping, decorating and baking cookies will be as pleasurable as it is savoring and sharing them with loved ones. With *The Ultimate Cookie Book*, you have everything you need to make cookies, squares and muffins that will win everyone's heart!

REFRIGERATOR COOKIES

With cookie dough in the refrigerator, you'll never be caught empty handed when a surprise visitor comes to the door. These cookies have the advantage of being partly prepared ahead of time and frozen. A few minutes are enough to get them ready for baking.

The delicious aroma that fills the house as they are baking will welcome anyone and everyone...who can resist these fresh and light delights?

GINGER SNAPS

(3 dozen)

½ cup	unsalted butter	125 mL
½ cup	granulated sugar	125 mL
2 tbsp	honey	30 mL
1	egg	1
1⅓ cups	all-purpose flour	325 mL
½ tsp	baking soda	2 mL
1 tsp	ground clove	5 mL
1 tsp	cinnamon	5 mL
1½ tsp	ground ginger	7 mL

- In a large bowl, cream butter with sugar. Add honey and egg; beat well. Sift together dry ingredients and add to batter.

- Knead dough until it holds together. Shape into a roll, about 1 inch (2.5 cm) in diameter. Wrap in waxed paper and chill overnight in refrigerator.

- Preheat oven to 350°F (180°C). Grease a cookie sheet.

- Cut dough into slices, about ¼ inch (5 mm) thick. With a knife, make small slits on the surface. Arrange slices on cookie sheet, about 2 inches (5 cm) apart. Bake 8 to 10 minutes, until cookies are light golden. Let cool before removing from cookie sheet.

ORANGE ICEBOX COOKIES

(3 dozen)

½ cup	unsalted butter, softened	125 mL
1 cup	granulated sugar	250 mL
1	egg	1
1 tbsp	grated orange rind	15 mL
1¾ cups	all-purpose flour	425 mL
¼ tsp	salt	1 mL
¼ tsp	baking soda	1 mL
¼ cup	granulated sugar	50 mL
	few drops each of yellow and red food coloring	

ICING

½ cup	confectioners' sugar	125 mL
2 tbsp	orange juice	30 mL

- In a large bowl, cream butter and sugar. Add egg and orange rind; mix well. Sift together flour, salt and baking soda; add to creamed mixture.

- On a floured board, knead dough until smooth. Shape into 2 rolls, about 1½ inches (4 cm) in diameter, and flatten the tops to make an oval shape. Wrap in waxed paper and chill overnight in the refrigerator.

- Preheat oven to 375°F (190°C). Grease and flour a cookie sheet.

- Add food coloring to ¼ cup (50 mL) granulated sugar. Roll dough in colored sugar and slice ¼ inch (5 mm) thick. Arrange on cookie sheet and bake 10 to 12 minutes.

- To prepare icing, mix confectioners' sugar with orange juice. When cookies are done, transfer to wire racks; brush cookies with icing and allow to cool.

BUTTERY APRICOT COOKIES
(3 dozen)

½ cup	**unsalted butter, softened**	125 mL
½ cup	**sifted confectioners' sugar**	125 mL
½ tsp	**vanilla extract**	2 mL
1	**egg**	1
1¼ cups	**sifted all-purpose flour**	300 mL
¼ cup	**chopped dried apricots**	50 mL
	pinch of salt	

- Place butter, confectioners' sugar and vanilla in a large bowl. Mix together thoroughly. Add beaten egg.
- Sift flour and salt over creamed mixture and blend in gradually, working dough by hand. Add chopped apricots and mix well.
- Shape dough into roll about 1½ inches (4 cm) in diameter. Wrap in waxed paper and refrigerate overnight.
- Preheat oven to 400°F (200°C). Lightly grease cookie sheets.
- Cut roll into ⅛ inch (3 mm) thick slices. Arrange on cookie sheets and bake 7 to 8 minutes, or until edges start to brown. Let cool on wire racks.

VANILLA SNAPS
(2 dozen)

¼ cup	unsalted butter, softened	50 mL
¼ cup	granulated sugar	50 mL
¼ cup	brown sugar	50 mL
1	egg	1
¼ tsp	vanilla extract	1 mL
1 cup	all-purpose flour	250 mL
½ tsp	baking soda	2 mL
	pinch of salt	

- In a bowl, cream together butter and both sugars. Add egg and vanilla; mix well.

- Sift together dry ingredients and stir into first mixture.

- Shape dough into a 2 inch (5 cm) square log, about 22 inches (55 cm) long. Chill 12 hours in refrigerator.

- Preheat oven to 400°F (200°C). Grease a cookie sheet.

- Cut dough into ¼ inch (5 mm) thick slices. Transfer to cookie sheet and bake 8 to 10 minutes. Let cool on wire racks.

TAHINI AND SESAME COOKIES
(4 dozen)

½ cup	unsalted butter	125 mL
½ cup	granulated sugar	125 mL
½ cup	brown sugar	125 mL
1	large egg, beaten	1
2 tbsp	tahini	30 mL
1¾ cups	all-purpose flour	425 mL
¼ tsp	salt	1 mL
½ tsp	baking soda	2 mL
½ cup	sesame seeds	125 mL

- In a large bowl, cream butter with both sugars. Beat in egg and tahini.

- Sift dry ingredients together. Stir into egg mixture. Fold in sesame seeds.

- Knead dough until smooth. Shape into 2 square logs, about 1½ inches (4 cm) on each side. Wrap in waxed paper and chill overnight in refrigerator.

- Preheat oven to 375°F (190°C). Grease and flour a cookie sheet.

- Slice dough into ¼ inch (5 mm) thick squares. Arrange on cookie sheet and bake 8 to 10 minutes. Transfer cookies to wire rack and let cool.

CHEDDAR AND HAZELNUT COOKIES
(3 dozen)

½ cup	unsalted butter, cut up	125 mL
2 tbsp	grated Parmesan cheese	30 mL
1 cup	grated aged cheddar cheese	250 mL
2	eggs	2
2 cups	all-purpose flour	500 mL
½ tsp	baking soda	2 mL
¼ tsp	Cayenne pepper	1 mL
½ cup	finely chopped hazelnuts	125 mL

- In a large bowl, beat together butter, both cheeses and eggs. Mix in flour, baking soda and Cayenne pepper.

- On a floured board, gently knead dough until smooth. Shape into 3 rolls and roll in chopped hazelnuts. Wrap tightly in aluminum foil and chill overnight in refrigerator.

- Preheat oven to 350°F (180°C). Grease a cookie sheet.

- Cut dough into ¼ inch (5 mm) slices. Arrange on cookie sheet, about 1½ inches (4 cm) apart, and bake 12 to 14 minutes until golden. Transfer to wire racks and let cool.

NEAPOLITAN COOKIES

(4 dozen)

¾ cup	vegetable shortening	175 mL
1 cup	granulated sugar	250 mL
1	egg	1
1 tsp	almond extract	5 mL
2 cups	all-purpose flour	500 mL
1 tsp	baking powder	5 mL
1 tbsp	vegetable shortening	15 mL
2 tbsp	cocoa powder	30 mL
½ tsp	raspberry or strawberry extract	2 mL
1	egg white, slightly beaten	1
	red food coloring	

- In a large bowl, cream ¾ cup (175 mL) shortening with sugar. Add egg and almond extract; mix well. Sift flour with baking powder. Blend into creamed mixture.

- Divide dough into 3 portions. To one, add 1 tbsp (15 mL) shortening and cocoa. To another, add a few drops of red food coloring and raspberry extract. Blend well.

- With plastic wrap, line a loaf pan, about 3 x 6 inches and 2 inches deep (7.5 x 15 x 5 cm). Press the chocolate dough into the bottom of the pan and brush with egg white. Place the white dough over the chocolate dough, press together and brush with egg white. Place the pink dough on top, press and brush with egg white. Wrap the plastic around the three layers to cover the whole package. Chill several hours in the refrigerator.

- Preheat oven to 375°F (190°C). Remove dough from loaf pan and cut into ¼ inch (5 mm) thick slices. Bake on ungreased sheet 10 to 12 minutes, or until firm. Transfer to wire racks and let cool.

Press the chocolate dough into the bottom of the pan and brush with egg white. Place the white dough over top, press together and brush with egg white.

Place the pink dough on top, press and brush with egg white.

Remove dough from loaf pan and cut into ¼ inch (5 mm) thick slices.

COCOA BUTTONS

(4 dozen)

⅓ cup	vegetable shortening	75 mL
¾ cup	packed brown sugar	175 mL
1	egg	1
2 tbsp	instant coffee crystals	30 mL
1 tbsp	hot water	15 mL
2 tbsp	cocoa powder	30 mL
1½ cups	all-purpose flour	375 mL

- In a large bowl, cream shortening with brown sugar. Add egg and beat well.
- Dissolve instant coffee in hot water and add to mixture. Add cocoa, then gradually add flour until well-mixed.
- Divide dough in two and shape each portion into a log about 2 inches (5 cm) in diameter. Wrap in plastic and refrigerate dough overnight.
- Preheat oven to 350°F (180°C); lightly grease cookie sheets.
- Slice dough into ¼ inch (5 mm) slices and place on cookie sheet. Using a plastic straw, press 2 or 4 holes into each circle.
- Bake 8 to 10 minutes until cookies become slightly firm. When done, transfer to wire racks and let cool. Store in an airtight container.

POPPY SEED COOKIES

(5 dozen)

1 cup	vegetable shortening	250 mL
¾ cup	granulated sugar	175 mL
1	egg	1
¼ cup	poppy seeds	50 mL
2 tbsp	yogurt	30 mL
1½ tsp	grated orange rind	7 mL
2½ cups	all-purpose flour	625 mL
½ tsp	baking powder	2 mL

- In a large bowl, cream shortening and sugar until fluffy. Add egg, poppy seeds, yogurt and orange rind; mix well.
- Sift flour with baking powder. Add to creamed mixture and mix well.
- Divide dough into 3 portions and shape into logs, about 2 inches (5 cm) in diameter. Wrap in plastic and chill 6 hours or overnight.
- Preheat oven to 350°F (180°C). Grease a cookie sheet.
- Cut logs into ¼ inch (5 mm) slices. Transfer to ungreased cookie sheet and bake 8 to 10 minutes.
- When done, transfer cookies to wire racks and let cool.

ORANGE PECAN DIAMONDS
(6 dozen)

¾ cup	vegetable oil	175 mL
1	egg	1
½ cup	brown sugar	125 mL
½ cup	granulated sugar	125 mL
2 tbsp	plain yogurt	30 mL
1 tbsp	grated orange rind	15 mL
1¼ cups	all-purpose flour	300 mL
1 tsp	baking soda	5 mL
1 cup	whole wheat flour	250 mL
½ cup	finely chopped pecans	125 mL

- In a large bowl, beat oil with egg. Beat in both sugars, yogurt and orange rind.

- Sift all-purpose flour with baking soda. Stir in whole wheat flour. Work into egg mixture along with pecans until well-combined. Wrap in waxed paper and chill 4 hours.

- Preheat oven to 350°F (180°C); lightly grease cookie sheets.

- Working with half the dough at a time, roll out each portion on floured board to ¼ inch (5 mm) thickness. Cut into diamonds about 2 inches (5 cm) long and 1 inch (2.5 cm) wide.

- Transfer to cookie sheets and bake 10 to 12 minutes until edges become slightly crisp. When done, transfer to wire racks and let cool.

ANISE BARS
(4 dozen)

¾ cup	unsalted butter	175 mL
¾ cup	granulated sugar	175 mL
1	egg	1
2 tbsp	anise seeds	30 mL
2 cups	all-purpose flour	500 mL

- Cream butter and sugar until fluffy. Add egg and anise seeds; mix well.

- Work in flour until evenly blended. Chill overnight.

- Preheat oven to 350°F (180°C); lightly grease cookie sheets.

- Roll dough out about ⅛ inch (3 mm) thick, and cut into bars about 1½ x 2½ inches (3.5 x 6 cm). Place on cookie sheets, about ½ inch (1 cm) apart, and bake for 10 to 12 minutes, or until edges start to brown.

- When done, transfer to wire racks and let cool.

MIXED-NUT COOKIES

(3 dozen)

1 cup	unsalted butter	250 mL
2 cups	brown sugar	500 mL
2	eggs, beaten	2
3½ cups	all-purpose flour	875 mL
1 tsp	baking soda	5 mL
1 cup	chopped mixed nuts	250 mL
	pinch of salt	

- In large bowl, cream butter with brown sugar. Add eggs and mix well.

- In a separate bowl, mix together flour, baking soda and salt. Gradually blend into batter, mixing well with wooden spoon. Mix in nuts.

- Divide dough in half and shape into 2 blocks or logs. Wrap in waxed paper and secure in foil. Refrigerate at least 12 hours.

- Preheat oven to 350°F (180°C). Grease and flour a cookie sheet.

- Cut dough into ¼ inch (5 mm) thick slices and arrange on cookie sheet. Bake 8 to 10 minutes. When done, carefully transfer cookies to wire rack and let cool.

NOTE: *Cookie dough will keep four to five days in the refrigerator.*

In large bowl, cream butter with brown sugar.

With a wooden spoon, gradually blend in flour mixed with baking soda and salt.

Add nuts and mix.

Divide dough in half and shape each portion into a flattened log.

CURRANT COOKIES
(2 dozen)

½ cup	unsalted butter	125 mL
½ cup	superfine sugar	125 mL
1	egg	1
1 tbsp	milk	15 mL
½ tsp	vanilla extract	2 mL
1½ cups	all-purpose flour	375 mL
1 tsp	baking powder	5 mL
¼ cup	currants, washed	50 mL
	pinch of salt	
	brown sugar	

- In a large bowl, cream together butter and superfine sugar. Add egg and mix well.

- In a small bowl, combine milk and vanilla.

- Sift together dry ingredients; add currants. Gradually stir into butter mixture, alternating with milk and vanilla.

- Shape dough into rolls about 2 inches (5 cm) in diameter; chill about 12 hours in refrigerator.

- Preheat oven to 350°F (180°C). Grease and flour a cookie sheet.

- Cut rolls into ¼ inch (5 mm) thick slices and transfer to cookie sheet. Sprinkle slices with brown sugar and bake about 10 minutes. Let cool on wire racks.

CHERRY ALMOND AND LEMON COOKIES

(3 dozen)

1 cup	unsalted butter	250 mL
2 cups	confectioners' sugar	500 mL
1	egg	1
2	egg yolks	2
3½ cups	cake flour	875 mL
¾ cup	chopped almonds	175 mL
¾ cup	coarsely chopped cherries	175 mL
	grated zest of 1 lemon	

- Cream together butter and confectioners' sugar. Add egg, egg yolks, lemon zest and then flour, mixing well after each addition. Fold in almonds and cherries, without kneading the dough too much. Divide into 2 portions.

- Line two greased pans, about 6 x 3 x 2 inches (15 x 7.5 x 5 cm), with plastic wrap, place dough in pans and refrigerate overnight.

- Preheat oven to 350°F (180°C). Grease and flour a cookie sheet.

- Remove dough from pan and cut into ½ inch (1 cm) thick rectangles. Transfer to cookie sheet and bake 10 to 12 minutes. Let cool on wire racks.

CORNMEAL AND NUTMEG COOKIES

(3 dozen)

¾ cup	granulated sugar	175 mL
¾ cup	unsalted butter, softened	175 mL
2	egg yolks	2
1¼ cups	all-purpose flour	300 mL
¾ cup	cornmeal	175 mL
1 tsp	baking powder	5 mL
¼ tsp	salt	1 mL
½ tsp	ground nutmeg	2 mL

- In a large bowl, beat sugar and butter with an electric mixer at medium speed. Add egg yolks and continue beating until light and fluffy.

- Beat in flour, cornmeal, baking powder, salt and nutmeg until dough is smooth.

- Divide dough into 2 portions. Shape each into a roll, about 2 inches (5 cm) in diameter. Wrap in plastic and chill in refrigerator at least 3 hours and up to 3 days. (Dough can also be frozen for up to 6 months.)

- Preheat oven to 350°F (180°C). Lightly grease a cookie sheet.

- Cut rolls into ¼ inch (5 mm) thick slices. Arrange flat on cookie sheet, about 2 inches (5 cm) apart. Bake 8 to 10 minutes until cookies are firm and edges are golden. Transfer to wire racks and let cool. Store in an airtight container.

DATE AND WHEAT GERM ICEBOX COOKIES

(3 dozen)

½ cup	unsalted butter	125 mL
1 cup	brown sugar	250 mL
2 tbsp	honey	30 mL
1	large egg, beaten	1
1½ cups	all-purpose flour	375 mL
½ tsp	baking soda	2 mL
¼ tsp	salt	1 mL
¾ cup	wheat germ	175 mL
⅔ cup	chopped dates	150 mL

- In a large bowl, cream butter with brown sugar. Beat in honey and egg. Sift flour with baking soda and salt. Mix into creamed mixture, along with wheat germ and dates.

- Shape dough into 2 logs, about 1½ inches (4 cm) in diameter, then mold sides to make logs triangular. Wrap in waxed paper then in foil. Refrigerate overnight.

- Preheat oven to 350°F (180°C). Grease and flour cookie sheet.

- Cut logs into ¼ inch (5 mm) thick slices and arrange on cookie sheet. Bake 8 to 10 minutes. Transfer cookies to wire racks and let cool.

MARBLED COOKIES

(3 dozen)

1	**square semi-sweet baking chocolate**	1
1½ cups	**all-purpose flour**	375 mL
¼ tsp	**salt**	1 mL
½ tsp	**baking powder**	2 mL
½ cup	**unsalted butter, softened**	125 mL
½ cup	**granulated sugar**	125 mL
1	**large egg**	1
½	**vanilla bean**	½

- Melt chocolate in top of double-boiler, over simmering water; set aside to cool slightly.

- In a bowl, mix flour, salt and baking powder; set aside.

- In a medium bowl, cream butter and sugar with an electric mixer at medium speed. Add egg and beat until light and fluffy.

- With a sharp knife, split vanilla bean lengthwise, scrape out seeds and add them to egg mixture. Stir in reserved dry ingredients.

- Divide dough in half and place 1 portion on a piece of waxed paper. Add melted chocolate to the other portion and mix until color is uniform. Roughly knead the 2 portions together on the waxed paper to make a marbled ball.

- Shape dough into two 6 inch (15 cm) long rolls, about 2 inches (5 cm) in diameter. Wrap tightly in waxed paper or plastic and chill overnight in refrigerator.

- Preheat oven to 375°F (190°C). Lightly grease a cookie sheet.

- Cut rolls of dough into ¼ inch (5 mm) slices and arrange on cookie sheet, about 1 inch (2.5 cm) apart. Bake on middle rack in oven 8 to 10 minutes; do not let cookies brown. Transfer to wire racks and let cool. Store in an airtight container or wrap tightly and freeze.

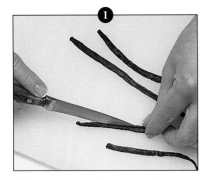

With a sharp knife, split vanilla bean lengthwise.

Scrape the inside.

Remove seeds.

ALMOND AND CINNAMON COOKIES

(3 dozen)

2 tbsp	vegetable shortening	30 mL
3 tbsp	unsalted butter	45 mL
¾ cup	brown sugar	175 mL
2	eggs, beaten	2
1⅓ cups	all-purpose flour	325 mL
½ tsp	baking soda	2 mL
1 tsp	cinnamon	5 mL
3 tbsp	chopped almonds	45 mL
	pinch of salt	

- In a large bowl, cream together shortening and butter. Stir in brown sugar and eggs.

- Sift together dry ingredients and blend into first mixture. Fold in almonds.

- Shape dough into 2 rolls, about 2 inches (5 cm) in diameter. Then mold sides to make rolls triangular. Chill 12 hours in refrigerator.

- Preheat oven to 400°F (200°C). Grease a cookie sheet.

- Cut dough into ¼ inch (5 mm) thick slices. Transfer to cookie sheet and bake 10 minutes.

DROP COOKIES

Drop cookies are 'dropped' by the spoonful onto the cookie sheet; hence the name. Why not use a small ice cream scoop to shape them? That way, when they are baked, the cookies will all have the same texture, shape and color.

In a pinch, you'll be happy to know that these are not only the easiest and quickest cookies to bake, but they also suit any occasion.

CANDIED GINGER DROPS
(2 dozen)

1½ cups	all-purpose flour	375 mL
½ tsp	salt	2 mL
½ tsp	baking soda	2 mL
½ cup	vegetable shortening	125 mL
¾ cup	granulated sugar	175 mL
½ cup	evaporated milk	125 mL
½ cup	chopped candied ginger	125 mL
	grated zest of 1 orange	

- Preheat oven to 375°F (190°C). Grease a cookie sheet.
- Sift flour with salt and baking soda; set aside.
- Cream shortening with sugar and beat until light. Add evaporated milk; mix well. Mix in orange zest and ginger.
- Drop spoonfuls of batter onto cookie sheet and bake 12 minutes. When done, carefully transfer cookies to wire rack and let cool.

COCONUT MACAROONS
(2 dozen)

2 cups	confectioners' sugar	500 mL
2½ cups	finely shredded coconut	625 mL
4	egg whites	4
½ cup	whipping cream	125 mL
1 tsp	vanilla extract	5 mL
	pinch of salt	

- Preheat oven to 325°F (160°C).
- In a bowl, combine confectioners' sugar and coconut. In a separate bowl, beat egg whites until stiff and add to coconut mixture.
- Whip cream until stiff peaks form. Gently fold into coconut mixture, along with vanilla and salt.
- Drop spoonfuls of batter onto non-stick cookie sheet. Bake 15 minutes, or until macaroons are golden brown. Broil 2 minutes if desired. Transfer to wire racks and let cool.

GOLDEN RAISIN AND PECAN COOKIES

(3 dozen)

1 cup	unsalted butter, softened	250 mL
1¾ cups	brown sugar	425 mL
3	large eggs	3
2 cups	golden raisins	500 mL
3 cups	all-purpose flour	750 mL
1 cup	chopped pecans	250 mL
2 tsp	baking soda	10 mL
2 tsp	cinnamon	10 mL
	pinch of salt	

- Preheat oven to 350°F (180°C). Grease and lightly flour cookie sheets.

- Cream butter in large bowl. Add brown sugar and blend well. Add eggs, one at a time, beating well between additions.

- Dust raisins with ¼ cup (50 mL) of flour. Add to egg mixture along with pecans; mix well.

- Sift remaining flour, baking soda, cinnamon and salt together. Stir into egg mixture; batter should be stiff.

- Drop medium spoonfuls of batter onto cookie sheets. Bake 15 minutes, or according to size, until golden brown.

- When done, transfer cookies to wire racks and let cool.

BRAZIL NUT AND ORANGE COOKIES

(3 dozen)

½ cup	unsalted butter	125 mL
1½ cups	granulated sugar	375 mL
2	eggs, beaten	2
2 cups	all-purpose flour	500 mL
1 tsp	baking powder	5 mL
¼ tsp	salt	1 mL
1 tbsp	grated orange rind	15 mL
⅓ cup	orange juice	75 mL
¼ tsp	lemon extract	1 mL
¼ cup	Brazil nuts	50 mL
¾ cup	finely chopped nuts	175 mL
	raisins (optional)	

ICING

1 cup	confectioners' sugar	250 mL
2 tbsp	water	30 mL
1 tsp	lemon juice	5 mL

- Preheat oven to 350°F (180°C). Grease a cookie sheet.

- In a large bowl, cream butter with sugar. Add eggs and mix well. Sift together dry ingredients and add to egg mixture. Mix in orange rind, orange juice and lemon extract. Fold in Brazil nuts and raisins, if desired.

- Drop spoonfuls of batter onto cookie sheet, 2 inches (5 cm) apart. Bake 10 to 12 minutes.

- Meanwhile, prepare icing: mix together confectioners' sugar, water and lemon juice. Spoon over hot cookies and sprinkle with chopped nuts; let cool.

COCONUT OATMEAL CRUNCHES
(2 dozen)

½ cup	unsalted butter	125 mL
½ cup	brown sugar	125 mL
1	egg	1
¾ cup	oatmeal flakes	175 mL
½ cup	shredded coconut	125 mL
1 cup	all-purpose flour	250 mL
⅛ tsp	baking soda	0.5 mL
1 tsp	baking powder	5 mL
	pinch of salt	

- Preheat oven to 325°F (160°C). Grease a cookie sheet.

- In a large bowl, cream butter. Beating constantly, add brown sugar, egg, oatmeal and coconut. Sift together remaining ingredients and add to oatmeal mixture; mix well.

- Drop spoonfuls of batter onto cookie sheet, 2 inches (5 cm) apart. Flatten lightly with a fork. Bake 12 to 15 minutes and broil 30 seconds, if desired.

*O*ATMEAL AND CINNAMON APPLE COOKIES

(3 dozen)

3	apples, cored, peeled and sliced	3
2 tbsp	superfine sugar	30 mL
¼ tsp	cinnamon	1 mL
1 cup	unsalted butter, softened	250 mL
1 cup	brown sugar	250 mL
½ cup	granulated sugar	125 mL
2	eggs	2
1 tsp	vanilla extract	5 mL
1¼ cups	all-purpose flour	300 mL
1 tsp	baking soda	5 mL
¼ tsp	salt	1 mL
½ tsp	ground nutmeg	2 mL
3 cups	oatmeal flakes	750 mL

- Preheat oven to 350°F (180°C). Lightly grease a cookie sheet.
- Place apples, superfine sugar and cinnamon in small saucepan. Cook over low heat until apples soften and mixture thickens. Remove from heat and set aside.
- In large bowl, cream butter with brown sugar and granulated sugar. Beat in eggs and vanilla.
- Sift together flour, baking soda, salt and nutmeg. Stir into egg mixture.
- Fold in oatmeal and apple mixture. Drop small spoonfuls of batter onto cookie sheet and bake 10 to 12 minutes.
- When done, carefully transfer cookies to wire racks and let cool.

Place apples, superfine sugar and cinnamon in small saucepan. Cook over low heat.

Sift together flour, baking soda, salt and nutmeg. Stir into egg mixture.

Fold in oatmeal and apple mixture.

PUMPKIN AND CURRANT COOKIES

(2 dozen)

½ cup	unsalted butter	125 mL
1 cup	brown sugar	250 mL
2	eggs	2
1¼ cups	pumpkin purée	300 mL
2 cups	cake flour	500 mL
1 tbsp	baking powder	15 mL
1 tsp	cinnamon	5 mL
¼ tsp	ground nutmeg	1 mL
¼ tsp	salt	1 mL
⅔ cup	currants	150 mL

- Preheat oven to 350°F (180°C). Grease a cookie sheet.

- In a large bowl, cream together butter and brown sugar. Add eggs and pumpkin; mix well. Blend in remaining ingredients.

- Drop spoonfuls of batter onto cookie sheet and bake 10 minutes. Let cool on wire racks.

CANDIED FRUIT COOKIES
(2½ dozen)

2½ cups	cake flour	625 mL
¼ tsp	salt	1 mL
¼ tsp	ground nutmeg	1 mL
¼ tsp	baking soda	1 mL
¾ cup	unsalted butter	175 mL
1 cup	granulated sugar	250 mL
1	egg	1
¼ cup	evaporated milk	50 mL
1 cup	chopped candied fruit	250 mL
	pinch of ground clove	

- Preheat oven to 375°F (190°C). Grease a cookie sheet.
- Sift flour with salt, nutmeg, baking soda and clove; set aside.
- Cream butter in large bowl. Add sugar and beat until well-blended. Beat in egg.
- Mix in half of reserved dry ingredients. Stir in evaporated milk, then remaining dry ingredients. Fold in candied fruit.
- Drop small spoonfuls of batter onto cookie sheet. Bake about 12 minutes.
- When done, carefully transfer cookies to wire rack and let cool.

Pineapple Rum Cookies
(2½ dozen)

2 cups	all-purpose flour	500 mL
1½ tsp	baking powder	7 mL
¼ tsp	salt	1 mL
¼ tsp	baking soda	1 mL
⅔ cup	vegetable shortening	150 mL
1 cup	brown sugar	250 mL
¼ cup	granulated sugar	50 mL
2	eggs	2
1 cup	chopped pineapple, well drained	250 mL
1 tsp	rum extract	5 mL

- Preheat oven to 400°F (200°C).

- Sift flour, baking powder, salt and baking soda together in small bowl; set aside.

- In large bowl, cream shortening. Add brown and granulated sugars; beat until smooth. Add eggs, one at a time, pineapple and rum extract, beating well after each addition. Mix in sifted dry ingredients, blending thoroughly.

- Drop very small spoonfuls of batter onto ungreased cookie sheet. Bake about 10 minutes. When done, carefully transfer cookies to wire rack and let cool.

MAPLE PECAN COOKIES
(2½ dozen)

1 cup	unsalted butter	250 mL
1½ cups	brown sugar*	375 mL
2	eggs	2
1 tsp	maple extract	5 mL
2⅓ cups	all-purpose flour	575 mL
1 tsp	baking soda	5 mL
½ tsp	salt	2 mL
½ tsp	baking powder	2 mL
3 tbsp	maple syrup	45 mL
1¼ cups	chopped pecans	300 mL

- Preheat oven to 400°F (200°C). Grease and flour a cookie sheet.
- Cream butter with brown sugar in large bowl. Beat until fluffy. Beat in eggs and maple extract.
- Sift together dry ingredients. Add to batter and mix well. Stir in maple syrup and pecans.
- Drop small spoonfuls of batter onto cookie sheet. Bake about 12 minutes, then carefully transfer cookies to wire rack and let cool.

* Or you can use granulated maple sugar.

PEANUT BUTTER MULTI-GRAIN COOKIES
(2 dozen)

½ cup	peanut butter	125 mL
2 tbsp	vegetable oil	30 mL
1 cup	brown sugar	250 mL
1	large egg, beaten	1
½ cup	all-purpose flour	125 mL
¼ tsp	salt	1 mL
½ tsp	baking soda	2 mL
¾ cup	multi-grain cereal, crushed	175 mL

- Preheat oven to 350°F (180°C).
- In large bowl, mix peanut butter with oil and brown sugar. Stir in egg.
- Sift flour with salt and baking soda. Mix into peanut butter mixture. Stir in multi-grain cereal.
- Drop small spoonfuls of batter onto ungreased cookie sheet. Flatten slightly with fork and bake 10 to 12 minutes.
- When done, carefuliy transfer cookies to wire rack and let cool.

SOFT VANILLA DROPS WITH CRANBERRIES

(4½ dozen)

¾ cup	unsalted butter, softened	175 mL
½ cup	firmly packed brown sugar	125 mL
½ cup	honey	125 mL
1	egg	1
1 tsp	vanilla extract	5 mL
2 cups	all-purpose flour	500 mL
¾ tsp	baking soda	4 mL
½ tsp	baking powder	2 mL
1 cup	chopped cranberries	250 mL
	confectioners' sugar	

- Preheat oven to 375°F (190°C). Grease and flour a cookie sheet.

- In a large bowl, combine butter, brown sugar, honey, egg and vanilla. Beat with an electric mixer at medium speed until smooth. Add dry ingredients, except for cranberries, and mix well. Fold in cranberries with a wooden spoon.

- Drop small spoonfuls of batter onto cookie sheet and bake 6 to 9 minutes, until cookies are golden. Transfer to wire racks and let cool. Sprinkle with confectioners' sugar, if desired.

BANANA AND WALNUT COOKIES
(3 dozen)

½ cup	vegetable shortening	125 mL
1 cup	granulated sugar	250 mL
2	eggs, beaten	2
3	bananas, mashed	3
1⅓ cups	oatmeal flakes	325 mL
¾ cup	chopped walnuts	175 mL
1½ cups	all-purpose flour	375 mL
¾ tsp	baking soda	4 mL
¼ tsp	ground nutmeg	1 mL
¾ tsp	salt	4 mL

- Preheat oven to 375°F (190°C). Grease and flour a cookie sheet.
- In a large bowl, cream shortening and stir in sugar. One after the other, add eggs, bananas, oats and walnuts, mixing well after each addition.
- Sift together remaining dry ingredients and blend into batter.
- Drop spoonfuls of batter onto cookie sheet and bake 10 to 12 minutes. Let cool on wire racks.

RAISIN AND MACADAMIA NUT COOKIES

(3 dozen)

2½ cups	all-purpose flour	625 mL
1 tsp	allspice	5 mL
1 tsp	cinnamon	5 mL
½ tsp	ground nutmeg	2 mL
¼ tsp	salt	1 mL
3	large eggs	3
1½ cups	granulated sugar	375 mL
½ tsp	baking soda	2 mL
3 tbsp	hot water	45 mL
½ cup	unsalted butter, softened	125 mL
¼ cup	vegetable shortening	50 mL
¾ cup	chopped macadamia nuts	175 mL
½ cup	chopped pecans	125 mL
¾ cup	Thompson or sultana raisins, chopped	175 mL

- Preheat oven to 375°F (190°C). Grease a cookie sheet.

- Sift flour with allspice, cinnamon, nutmeg and salt. Repeat and set aside.

- Place eggs in large bowl and add granulated sugar. Blend well. In small bowl, mix baking soda with hot water; stir into egg mixture.

- One after the other, blend in butter, shortening, sifted dry ingredients, nuts and raisins.

- Drop 2 tbsp (30 mL) of batter for each cookie onto cookie sheet, about 2 inches (5 cm) apart. Bake about 12 minutes.

- When done, carefully transfer cookies to wire rack and let cool.

In a large bowl, beat eggs with sugar.

Blend in butter and shortening, then sifted dry ingredients.

Blend in nuts and raisins.

FRUITY OATMEAL COOKIES
(3 dozen)

1 cup	unsalted butter, softened	250 mL
1 cup	brown sugar	250 mL
½ cup	granulated sugar	125 mL
2	large eggs	2
2 tbsp	light cream	30 mL
1 tsp	vanilla extract	5 mL
2½ cups	all-purpose flour	625 mL
½ tsp	baking soda	2 mL
⅓ cup	chopped dried apricots	75 mL
⅓ cup	chopped dried papaya	75 mL
⅓ cup	chopped dried pineapple	75 mL
3 tbsp	all-purpose flour	45 mL
2 cups	oatmeal flakes	500 mL
	pinch of salt	
	pinch of cinnamon	
	pinch of ground nutmeg	

- Preheat oven to 375°F (190°C). Grease and flour a cookie sheet.
- In large bowl, cream butter with both sugars. Beat in eggs, cream and vanilla.
- Sift 2½ cups (625 mL) flour together with baking soda, salt, cinnamon and nutmeg. Stir into egg mixture.
- Dredge dried fruits in remaining flour and fold into batter, along with oats.
- Drop 2 tbsp (30 mL) of batter per cookie onto cookie sheet and flatten with a spoon. Bake 10 to 12 minutes or until edges are lightly browned.
- When done, carefully transfer cookies to wire rack and let cool.

*O*ATMEAL RAISIN COOKIES

(2 dozen)

⅓ cup	vegetable shortening	75 mL
1 cup	brown sugar	250 mL
1	large egg	1
1¼ cups	all-purpose flour	300 mL
1 tsp	baking powder	5 mL
¼ tsp	salt	1 mL
¼ cup	milk	50 mL
1 cup	oatmeal flakes	250 mL
½ cup	raisins	125 mL
½ cup	chopped walnuts	125 mL

- Preheat oven to 375°F (190°C).
- In a large bowl, cream shortening with brown sugar. Beat in egg until smooth.
- Sift flour, baking powder and salt over batter. Mix with wooden spoon or hand mixer.
- Pour in milk and continue mixing. Add oatmeal, raisins and walnuts. Mix to distribute evenly.
- Drop small spoonfuls of batter onto ungreased cookie sheets. Bake 10 to 12 minutes.
- When done, transfer cookies to wire racks and let cool.

Cutout Cookies

Cutout cookies are a real treat, for both the eye and the palate. What's more, for a lot of people, they bring back fond childhood memories. With a variety of cookie cutters to choose from, all you have to do is follow the recipe and be creative. As long as you let the dough chill an hour or two so that it is firm, you're sure to make great cookies each and every time.

These cookies, whether iced, decorated or left plain, will always hold a special place at a child's party or any other occasion.

GINGERBREAD COOKIES
(3 dozen)

1 cup	unsalted butter	250 mL
1 cup	granulated sugar	250 mL
1 cup	molasses	250 mL
½ cup	brown sugar	125 mL
1	egg	1
4 cups	all-purpose flour	1 L
1 tsp	baking soda	5 mL
½ tsp	ground ginger	2 mL
½ tsp	ground clove	2 mL
¾ cup	plain or flavored yogurt	175 mL
½ tsp	vanilla extract	2 mL
	pinch of salt	

- In a large bowl, cream butter. Stir in sugar, molasses and brown sugar. Add egg and beat until mixture is fluffy.
- Sift together flour, salt, baking soda and spices. Add these ingredients to the first mixture and blend. Stir in yogurt and vanilla extract.
- Shape dough into a large ball and chill at least 12 hours in refrigerator.
- Preheat oven to 350°F (180°C). Grease a cookie sheet.
- Lightly flour a board and sprinkle it with sugar; roll dough ¼ inch (5 mm) thick. Shape cookies with a cookie cutter and transfer to cookie sheet.
- Bake 12 to 15 minutes in oven. Let cool on wire racks.

COCONUT-TOPPED COOKIES
(2 dozen)

1 cup	unsalted butter, softened	250 mL
1 cup	brown sugar	250 mL
2	small eggs	2
1 tsp	vanilla extract	5 mL
½ tsp	rum flavoring	2 mL
2½ cups	flour, sifted	625 mL
1 tsp	baking powder	5 mL
	pinch of salt	
	sweetened finely shredded coconut	

- In a large bowl, cream together butter and brown sugar. Mix in eggs, vanilla and rum flavoring.

- Mix flour with baking powder and salt; add to batter and mix well. Cover with plastic wrap and chill 2 hours in refrigerator.

- Preheat oven to 375°F (190°C). Grease and flour a cookie sheet.

- Roll dough evenly on lightly floured surface. Shape cookies with cookie cutter and arrange on cookie sheet. Top cookies with shredded coconut and press down gently.

- Bake 10 to 12 minutes. When done, carefully transfer cookies to wire rack and let cool.

CARDAMOM COOKIES

(3 dozen)

⅓ cup	**vegetable shortening**	75 mL
¾ cup	**granulated sugar**	175 mL
1	**egg**	1
1 tbsp	**orange juice**	15 mL
1 tsp	**ground cardamom**	5 mL
½ tsp	**cinnamon**	2 mL
1½ cups	**all-purpose flour**	375 mL
ICING		
1 cup	**confectioners' sugar**	250 mL
2-3 tbsp	**lemon juice**	30-45 mL

- Preheat oven to 375°F (190°C). Lightly grease cookie sheets.

- In a large bowl, cream shortening with sugar. Add egg and juice; beat well.

- Add cardamom and cinnamon. Gradually mix in flour.

- Working with half the dough at a time, roll out on floured board, ⅛ inch (3 mm) thick. Cut into different shapes and arrange on cookie sheet. Bake 8 to 10 minutes, until just beginning to brown. Transfer cookies to wire racks and let cool.

- Combine icing ingredients and place in a pastry bag. Decorate cookies and store in an airtight container.

*O*ATMEAL SHORTBREAD
(2 dozen)

½ cup	butter	125 mL
¾ cup	granulated sugar	175 mL
1	egg	1
¼ cup	honey	50 mL
2 tbsp	plain yogurt	30 mL
1 tsp	cinnamon	5 mL
¼ tsp	allspice	1 mL
2 cups	all-purpose flour	500 mL
1 cup	oatmeal	250 mL
2 tsp	baking powder	10 mL

- Preheat oven to 350°F (180°C). Lightly grease cookie sheets.

- In a large bowl, cream butter with sugar until light and fluffy. Add egg, honey, yogurt, cinnamon and allspice, blending well after each addition.

- Combine flour, oatmeal and baking powder. Add to butter mixture, blending in the last of the dry ingredients with a wooden spoon.

- Place dough on floured board and knead a few times until smooth.

- Divide into 3 portions. Roll each portion into a circle about 6 inches (15 cm) in diameter.

- With your fingers, crimp the edges of each circle. With a knife, score the surface of the dough into 8 wedges per circle; prick with a fork. Using 2 spatulas, transfer circles to cookie sheet.

- Bake 18 to 20 minutes, until circles start to brown. Remove from oven and separate wedges. Transfer to wire rack and let cool completely.

*N*OTE: *You can make oatmeal by pulverizing rolled oats in a blender or food processor.*

With your fingers, crimp the edges of each circle.

With a knife, score the surface of the dough to make 8 wedges.

Prick with a fork.

MOLASSES ROUNDS
(2 dozen)

1 cup	unsalted butter	250 mL
1 cup	granulated sugar	250 mL
1	egg	1
2 tsp	baking soda	10 mL
1 cup	molasses	250 mL
¼ tsp	cinnamon	1 mL
¼ tsp	ground clove	1 mL
1 tsp	salt	5 mL
2 tsp	ground ginger	10 mL
1 tsp	dry mustard	5 mL
5 cups	all-purpose flour	1.25 L
⅔ cup	strong coffee, cold	150 mL

- Preheat oven to 350°F (180°C). Grease a cookie sheet.

- In a large bowl, cream together butter and sugar. Stir in egg. In another bowl, mix together baking soda and molasses; stir into first mixture.

- Blend in cinnamon, clove, salt, ginger and dry mustard. Sift flour and gradually add to batter, alternating with coffee.

- Roll dough out ½ inch (1 cm) thick. Shape into cookies with a round cookie cutter about 3 inches (8 cm) in diameter. Place rounds on cookie sheet and make crisscross patterns with a fork, if desired. Bake about 15 minutes. Let cool on wire racks.

TEA BISCUITS
(2 dozen)

⅔ cup	unsalted butter	150 mL
⅔ cup	granulated sugar	150 mL
1	egg, beaten	1
½ tsp	choice of flavoring (vanilla, almond, etc.)	2 mL
2 cups	all-purpose flour	500 mL
½ tsp	baking soda	2 mL
1½ tsp	cream of tartar	7 mL
¼ tsp	salt	1 mL
	sugar	

- Preheat oven to 350°F (180°C). Grease a cookie sheet.

- In a large bowl, cream butter. Mixing constantly, gradually add sugar, then egg, then flavoring.

- Sift together dry ingredients and add to first mixture to make a firm dough.

- Roll dough out ½ inch (1 cm) thick. Shape biscuits with a cookie cutter and transfer to cookie sheet. Prick with a fork; sprinkle with sugar, if desired. Bake 10 to 12 minutes. Let cool on wire racks.

OCHA THINS

(4 dozen)

⅓ cup	vegetable shortening	75 mL
¾ cup	granulated sugar	175 mL
1	egg	1
1 tbsp	cold espresso coffee	15 mL
1½ cups	all-purpose flour	375 mL
2 tbsp	instant coffee crystals	30 mL
1 tsp	cinnamon	5 mL
	coffee beans	

- Preheat oven to 375°F (190°C).

- In a large bowl, cream shortening with sugar. Add egg and espresso coffee; beat well.

- Combine flour, instant coffee crystals and cinnamon. Gradually stir into egg mixture, working the last bit in by hand, until dough becomes smooth and elastic.

- Working with half the dough at a time, roll out on floured board as thinly as possible. Cut into 2 inch (5 cm) circles with fluted edges.

- Transfer to ungreased cookie sheets and put a coffee bean in the center of each cookie. Bake for 8 to 10 minutes until beginning to brown at edges. Transfer to wire racks and let cool.

Maple Brittle Cookies

(2½ dozen)

½ cup	maple syrup	125 mL
3 tbsp	unsalted butter	45 mL
⅓ cup	whole almonds, with skin	75 mL
3 cups	all-purpose flour	750 mL
2 tsp	baking powder	10 mL
¼ tsp	salt	1 mL
⅔ cup	unsalted butter	150 mL
1 cup	granulated sugar	250 mL
2	large eggs, beaten	2

- In a saucepan, heat maple syrup and 3 tbsp (45 mL) butter over medium heat, about 15 minutes. Add almonds and increase temperature to high. Pour into a mold and let harden in the refrigerator. Break into small pieces in a food processor.

- Sift together flour, baking powder and salt; set aside.

- In a large bowl, cream ⅔ cup (150 mL) butter with sugar. Add egg and sifted dry ingredients, mixing well to obtain a smooth dough. Cover and chill 2 hours in refrigerator.

- Preheat oven to 375°F (190°C). Grease a cookie sheet.

- Divide dough in half and roll each portion separately on lightly floured surface, about ¼ inch (5 mm) thick. Using cookie cutters, cut out various shapes and transfer to cookie sheet.

- Sprinkle cookies with maple brittle and bake about 8 minutes. Transfer cookies to wire rack and let cool.

Coconut and Walnut
OATMEAL COOKIES
(2 dozen)

⅓ cup	vegetable shortening	75 mL
⅓ cup	granulated sugar	75 mL
¾ cup	brown sugar	175 mL
1	egg, beaten	1
½ tsp	vanilla extract	2 mL
1 cup	oatmeal flakes	250 mL
¾ cup	all-purpose flour	175 mL
½ tsp	baking powder	2 mL
½ tsp	baking soda	2 mL
½ tsp	salt	2 mL
½ cup	chopped walnuts	125 mL
½ cup	shredded coconut	125 mL

- Preheat oven to 350°F (180°C). Lightly grease a cookie sheet.

- In a bowl, cream the shortening. Add both sugars and mix well. Add egg, vanilla, oatmeal, all-purpose flour, baking powder, baking soda and salt; mix well. Fold in walnuts and coconut.

- Knead dough well, and roll out on a lightly floured surface about ¾ inch (2 cm) thick. Shape into cookies with a round cookie cutter about 2½ inches (6 cm) in diameter. Transfer to cookie sheet and bake 12 to 15 minutes. Let cool on wire racks.

In a bowl, cream the shortening. Add both sugars and mix well.

Add oatmeal, all-purpose flour, baking powder, baking soda and salt; mix well.

Fold in walnuts and coconut.

MALTED BUTTER COOKIES

(2 dozen)

½ cup	unsalted butter	125 mL
¾ cup	confectioners' sugar	175 mL
1	egg	1
1 tsp	vanilla extract	5 mL
1 tsp	malt extract	5 mL
2 cups	cake flour	500 mL
	milk	
	coarse sugar	

- In a large bowl, cream butter with sugar. Mix in egg, vanilla, malt then flour. Chill 1 hour in refrigerator.
- Preheat oven to 350°F (180°C). Lightly grease a cookie sheet.
- On a floured board, roll dough ⅛ inch (3 mm) thick. Shape cookies with a 2½ inch (6 cm) square cookie cutter with a serrated edge.
- Arrange on cookie sheet, brush with milk and sprinkle with coarse sugar. Bake about 8 minutes, then transfer to wire racks and let cool.

ALMOND RINGS

(3 dozen)

⅔ cup	vegetable shortening	150 mL
1 cup	brown sugar	250 mL
2	eggs, beaten	2
¼ tsp	vanilla extract	1 mL
2½ cups	all-purpose flour	625 mL
1½ tsp	baking powder	7 mL
¼ cup	milk	50 mL
¼ cup	slivered almonds	50 mL
	pinch of salt	

- Preheat oven to 400°F (200°C). Grease a cookie sheet.
- In a large bowl, cream shortening. Add brown sugar, eggs, then vanilla, mixing well after each addition. Sift together dry ingredients and stir into egg mixture.
- On a lightly floured board, roll dough ¼ inch (5 mm) thick. Shape cookies with a round cookie cutter with a serrated edge, about 3 inches (7.5 cm) in diameter. Use a smaller cookie cutter to cut out the center of each cookie.
- Arrange rings on cookie sheet, brush with milk and sprinkle with slivered almonds. Bake 8 to 10 minutes. Let cool on wire racks.

BRIDGE COOKIES

(4 dozen)

⅓ cup	vegetable shortening	75 mL
¾ cup	granulated sugar	175 mL
1	egg	1
1 tbsp	lemon juice	15 mL
1¼ cups	all-purpose flour	300 mL
2 tbsp	cocoa powder	30 mL
2 tbsp	all-purpose flour	30 mL
	red food coloring	
	chocolate sprinkles and red colored sugar	

- Preheat oven to 375°F (190°C). Lightly grease cookie sheets.

- In a large bowl, cream shortening with sugar. Add egg and lemon juice; beat well. Gradually add flour and mix well. Add a few drops of red coloring.

- Divide dough into 2 portions. To one, mix in cocoa, to the other, add 2 tbsp (30 mL) flour. Knead dough a few times until smooth and elastic.

- Roll each portion out on floured board as thinly as possible. Cut pink portion into hearts and diamonds. Cut chocolate portion into clubs and spades.

- Transfer to cookie sheets. Lightly sprinkle red colored sugar on pink cookies, and chocolate sprinkles or cocoa on brown cookies.

- Bake 8 to 10 minutes, until just beginning to harden. Do not let cookies brown. Transfer to wire racks and let cool. Store in an airtight container.

Add a few drops of red coloring to the dough and mix in.

To one portion, mix in cocoa, to the other, add 2 tbsp (30 mL) flour.

Lightly sprinkle red colored sugar on pink cookies.

WHEAT BRAN CRACKERS
(3 dozen)

4 tbsp	**vegetable shortening**	60 mL
¼ cup	**brown sugar**	50 mL
¼ cup	**honey**	50 mL
2 tbsp	**molasses**	30 mL
1	**egg**	1
1 tsp	**vanilla extract**	5 mL
¾ cup	**whole wheat flour**	175 mL
1 cup	**all-purpose flour**	250 mL
¼ cup	**wheat bran**	50 mL

- Preheat oven to 350°F (180°C). Lightly grease a cookie sheet.

- In a small bowl, beat shortening, brown sugar, honey, molasses, egg and vanilla until smooth. Sift both flours and add to egg mixture along with wheat bran. Mix into a firm dough.

- On a floured board, knead dough until smooth. Roll dough ⅛ inch (3 mm) thick, then cut into 2½ inch (6 cm) squares.

- Arrange squares on cookie sheet, 1½ inches (4 cm) apart and prick with toothpick. Bake about 10 minutes until golden. Let cool on cookie sheet.

SHAPED COOKIES

Let your imagination run wild! Pinwheels, crescents, pretzels, braids, wind-mills...there's no limit to the shapes you can make. Because the dough is generally rich in butter or shortening, it is a good idea to refrigerate it before handling, so that it becomes less sticky.

Invite young and old alike to mold cookies. Not only will they have fun, but the results are scrumptious and pleasing to the eye as well!

PIZZELLES
(3½ dozen)

¾ cup	unsalted butter, melted	175 mL
¾ cup	granulated sugar	175 mL
4	eggs, lightly beaten	4
½ tsp	vanilla extract	2 mL
2 cups	all-purpose flour	500 mL
2 tsp	baking powder	10 mL
⅛ tsp	salt	0.5 mL

- Grease pizzelle iron and heat it according to manufacturer's directions. In a large bowl, mix butter with sugar; beat in eggs and vanilla. Mix flour with baking powder and salt; stir into egg mixture.

- Drop 1 tbsp (15 mL) of batter onto iron and close. Bake about 30 seconds until golden brown. Carefully remove from iron and let cool; repeat with remaining batter.

LEMON-LIME TWISTS
(4½ dozen)

1 cup	unsalted butter, softened	250 mL
¾ cup	granulated sugar	175 mL
1	egg	1
1 tsp	lemon extract	5 mL
1 tsp	grated lime rind	5 mL
2 tbsp	milk	30 mL
¼ tsp	salt	1 mL
2½ cups	all-purpose flour	625 mL
½ cup	confectioners' sugar	125 mL
2 tsp	lemon juice	10 mL

- Preheat oven to 350°F (180°C). Grease a cookie sheet.

- In a large bowl, beat butter and sugar until light and fluffy. Add egg, lemon extract and lime rind; mix well. Mix in milk, salt, then flour, 1 cup (250 mL) at a time, blending well after each addition. Form dough into a ball and let stand 5 minutes.

- Divide dough in two and put 1 portion in the refrigerator until ready to use. Take some of the other portion and roll on a floured board into a 10 inch (25 cm) long rope. Fold rope in two and twist one rope around the other. Repeat with remaining dough.

- Arrange twists on cookie sheet, 1 inch (2.5 cm) apart. Bake 10 to 12 minutes, until golden. Transfer to wire racks.

- Meanwhile, mix confectioners' sugar with lemon juice. Brush over twists while still hot and let cool.

RASPBERRY WALNUT WINDMILLS

(2 dozen)

¾ cup	brown sugar	175 mL
½ cup	unsalted butter, softened	125 mL
½ cup	vegetable shortening	125 mL
½ tsp	vanilla extract	2 mL
1	egg	1
2 cups	all-purpose flour	500 mL
1 tsp	baking powder	5 mL
⅛ tsp	salt	0.5 mL
	raspberry jam	

WALNUT FILLING

¼ cup	brown sugar	50 mL
¼ cup	finely chopped walnuts	50 mL
1 tbsp	unsalted butter	15 mL

- In a large bowl, mix together brown sugar, butter, shortening, vanilla and egg. Stir in flour, baking powder and salt. Cover and chill 1 hour in refrigerator until firm.

- Meanwhile, prepare filling: mix together brown sugar, walnuts and butter; set aside.

- Preheat oven to 375°F (190°C). Divide dough in half and roll each on a floured board into a rectangle, about ⅛ inch (3 mm) thick.

- Cut dough into 3 inch (7.5 cm) squares. Arrange on an ungreased cookie sheet, 2 inches (5 cm) apart. Cut squares diagonally from each corner almost to the center. Place 1 tbsp (15 mL) of jam in the center of half the squares; place 1 tbsp (15 mL) walnut filling in the center of the other half. Fold 4 points in towards the center to make windmills.

- Bake 6 to 8 minutes. Transfer to wire racks and let cool.

Cut dough into 3 inch (7.5 cm) squares.

Cut squares diagonally, from each corner almost to the center.

Place 1 tbsp (15 mL) of jam in the center of half the squares. Fold 4 points in towards the center to make windmills.

PEANUT BUTTER COOKIES

(2½ dozen)

½ cup	unsalted butter	125 mL
½ cup	brown sugar	125 mL
½ cup	granulated sugar	125 mL
½ cup	peanut butter	125 mL
1	small egg	1
1 cup	all-purpose flour	250 mL
¼ tsp	salt	1 mL
¼ tsp	baking soda	1 mL
	pinch of ground nutmeg	

- Preheat oven to 350°F (180°C). Lightly grease a cookie sheet.

- Cream butter in large bowl. Add both sugars and mix well. Add peanut butter and mix until smooth. Mix in egg.

- Combine remaining dry ingredients; blend into batter.

- Lightly dust hands with flour and shape dough into 1 inch (2.5 cm) balls. Arrange on cookie sheet and gently flatten with fork.

- Bake 10 to 15 minutes or until edges start to brown. When done, carefully transfer cookies to wire rack and let cool.

CHOCO-MINT PINWHEELS
(3 dozen)

1	square unsweetened baking chocolate	1
½ cup	unsalted butter	125 mL
½ cup	vegetable shortening	125 mL
1 cup	granulated sugar	250 mL
1	egg	1
1 tsp	mint flavoring	5 mL
2 cups	all-purpose flour	500 mL
1	egg white, lightly beaten	1
	green food coloring	

- Melt chocolate in top of double-boiler and set aside.

- In a large bowl, cream butter and shortening with sugar. Add egg and mint flavoring; mix well. Gradually mix in flour.

- Divide dough into 2 portions. To the first portion, add a few drops of green food coloring and blend well. To the second, add melted chocolate and blend well. Wrap each portion in waxed paper and chill in refrigerator about 1 hour, or until firm enough to roll.

- Roll each portion on floured waxed paper into a rectangle about 10 x 12 inches (25 x 30 cm), ¼ inch (5 mm) thick.

- Brush one rectangle with some of egg white. Lifting by the waxed paper, carefully place second rectangle on top of first, and gently press together. Trim edges to make an even rectangle, and brush top with remaining egg white.

- Starting from the long end, use waxed paper to roll dough. Wrap in waxed paper and transfer roll to refrigerator. Chill until firm, about 3 hours.

- Preheat oven to 375°F (190°C); lightly grease a cookie sheet.

- Cut roll into ¼ inch (5 mm) slices, discarding irregular end pieces. Transfer to cookie sheet and bake 10 to 12 minutes, until they start to firm. When done, transfer to wire racks and let cool.

PETITS FOURS
(3 dozen)

½ cup	unsalted butter	125 mL
½ cup	vegetable shortening	125 mL
¾ cup	granulated sugar	175 mL
½ cup	almond paste	125 mL
3	medium eggs	3
2½ cups	all-purpose flour	625 mL
1 tsp	choice of flavoring	5 mL
¾ cup	quartered maraschino cherries	175 mL

- Preheat oven to 350°F (180°C). Grease and flour a cookie sheet.

- Cream together butter, shortening and sugar. Mix in almond paste, eggs (one by one), then flour and flavoring.

- With a fluted no. 6 cookie press, squeeze cookies onto cookie sheet and decorate each with a quarter cherry.

- Bake about 10 minutes, or until lightly browned, and transfer gently to a wire rack; let cool.

𝒫ISTACHIO CRANBERRY COOKIES

(4 dozen)

1 cup	unsalted butter, softened	250 mL
1 cup	granulated sugar	250 mL
1	large egg, beaten	1
2 cups	all-purpose flour	500 mL
1 tsp	baking soda	5 mL
1 tsp	cream of tartar	5 mL
½ cup	chopped pistachios	125 mL
½ cup	dried cranberries	125 mL

- Preheat oven to 375°F (190°C). Grease and lightly flour cookie sheets.

- Cream butter and sugar together in large bowl. Beat in egg until smooth.

- Sift together flour, baking soda and cream of tartar; blend into creamed mixture. Add pistachios and cranberries; mix well.

- Shape dough into small balls and arrange on cookie sheets. Flatten with fork dipped in granulated sugar.

- Bake about 12 to 15 minutes, or according to size. When done, carefully transfer to wire racks and let cool.

MACAROONS
(3 dozen)

2 cups	blanched almonds	500 mL
1¼ cups	granulated sugar	300 mL
1 tbsp	grated lime rind	15 mL
2	egg whites, beaten with fork	2
	confectioners' sugar	

᧖

- Preheat oven to 375°F (190°C). Grease and flour a cookie sheet.

- Place almonds in food processor; grind into a fine powder. Add all remaining ingredients, except confectioners' sugar, and mix until well-blended.

- Shape dough into 1½ inch (4 cm) balls and arrange about 2 inches (5 cm) apart on cookie sheet. Flatten lightly with hands and let stand 10 minutes.

- Place in oven and bake 20 minutes. When done, press cookies gently together, two by two, back to back. Carefully transfer cookies to wire rack, let cool and dust with confectioners' sugar before serving.

Place almonds in food processor; grind into a fine powder. Add all remaining ingredients, except confectioners' sugar.

Shape dough into 1½ inch (4 cm) balls and arrange about 2 inches (5 cm) apart on cookie sheet.

Flatten lightly with your hand.

While still hot, press cookies gently together, two by two, back to back.

*O*ATMEAL RAISIN COCONUT COOKIES

(2 dozen)

⅓ cup	margarine	75 mL
½ cup	granulated sugar	125 mL
2	eggs	2
1¼ cups	all-purpose flour	300 mL
1¼ cups	oatmeal flakes	300 mL
1 cup	raisins	250 mL
¾ cup	shredded coconut	175 mL
1 tsp	baking powder	5 mL
1 tsp	baking soda	5 mL
1 tsp	cinnamon	5 mL
½ tsp	salt	2 mL
4 tbsp	milk	60 mL

6

- Preheat oven to 350°F (180°C). Grease a cookie sheet.

- In a large bowl, beat together margarine, sugar and eggs. In another bowl, mix together dry ingredients, and gradually add to egg mixture, alternating with milk.

- Shape dough into little balls and place on cookie sheet. Bake about 12 minutes. Let cool on wire racks.

ALMOND RUM CRESCENTS
(2½ dozen)

1 cup	unsalted butter, softened	250 mL
⅔ cup	confectioners' sugar, sifted	150 mL
1 tsp	vanilla extract	5 mL
½ tsp	rum extract	2 mL
1 cup	chopped almonds	250 mL
2½ cups	sifted all-purpose flour	625 mL
	pinch of salt	

- Preheat oven to 350°F (180°C).

- Cream butter with confectioners' sugar, vanilla and rum extract. Mix well and incorporate almonds, flour and salt. Knead dough until well-blended.

- Divide dough in two and roll each portion into a log, about 1 inch (2.5 cm) in diameter. Cut into 1 inch (2.5 cm) thick slices and arrange on ungreased cookie sheet. Shape into crescents and bake about 18 minutes.

- When done, carefully transfer crescents to wire rack and let cool. Dust with confectioners' sugar before serving.

ROGOLACH
(32 pieces)

½ cup	unsalted butter	125 mL
4 oz	cream cheese	125 g
¾ cup	granulated sugar	175 mL
1	egg yolk	1
2¼ cups	all-purpose flour	550 mL
½ tsp	baking powder	2 mL
1	egg white, lightly beaten	1
	apricot jelly	
	very finely chopped almonds	

- In a large bowl, cream butter and cream cheese with sugar. Add egg yolk.

- Sift flour with baking powder. Add to creamed mixture. Chill dough overnight in refrigerator.

- Preheat oven to 375°F (190°C); lightly grease cookie sheets.

- Divide dough into 4 portions. While rolling one portion, keep remainder chilled. On floured board, roll dough into a circle about ⅛ inch (3 mm) thick and 8 inches (20 cm) in diameter.

- Spread jelly over each circle. Cut into 8 wedges and roll up, starting at wide edge. Transfer to cookie sheet, with point of roll underneath. Brush with egg white and sprinkle with almonds.

- Bake 12 to 15 minutes, or until golden. When done, transfer to wire racks and let cool.

CHERRY COOKIES

(2 dozen)

1 cup	all-purpose flour	250 mL
½ tsp	baking powder	2 mL
½ tsp	baking soda	2 mL
¼ tsp	salt	1 mL
½ cup	vegetable shortening	125 mL
½ cup	granulated sugar	125 mL
1	egg, beaten	1
2 tbsp	milk	30 mL
½ tsp	vanilla extract	2 mL
½ cup	chopped dates	125 mL
½ cup	maraschino cherries, quartered	125 mL
1⅓ cups	corn flakes, crumbled	325 mL
3 tbsp	quartered maraschino cherries	45 mL

- Preheat oven to 375°F (190°C). Lightly grease a cookie sheet.
- Sift flour, baking powder, baking soda and salt into a large bowl. In another bowl, cream shortening with sugar. Add egg, milk and vanilla; mix well.
- Stir egg mixture into dry ingredients; fold in dates and ½ cup (125 mL) maraschino cherries.
- Shape dough into small balls, coat with corn flakes and place on cookie sheet, 1½ inches (4 cm) apart. Decorate cookies with remaining cherries.
- Bake 10 to 12 minutes; let cool before serving.

LEMON-LIME CRISPS
(3 dozen)

1 cup	vegetable shortening	250 mL
½ cup	granulated sugar	125 mL
½ cup	brown sugar	125 mL
1	large egg	1
¼ tsp	vanilla extract	1 mL
2 tsp	lime juice	10 mL
1 tbsp	grated lemon rind	15 mL
1 tsp	grated lime rind	5 mL
2½ cups	all-purpose flour	625 mL
½ tsp	baking soda	2 mL
½ tsp	salt	2 mL
	coarse sugar	

- Cream shortening with both sugars in large bowl. Beat in egg, vanilla, lime juice and grated lemon and lime rind.

- Sift flour with baking soda and salt. Add to batter and mix well. Chill dough 3 hours in refrigerator.

- Preheat oven to 375°F (190°C).

- Shape dough into triangles and arrange on ungreased cookie sheet. Flatten and sprinkle with coarse sugar. Bake 10 to 12 minutes, then carefully transfer cookies to wire rack and let cool.

MAPLE WALNUT PINWHEELS

(4 dozen)

¾ cup	butter	175 mL
¾ cup	granulated sugar	175 mL
1	egg	1
½ tsp	maple extract	2 mL
1¼ cups	all-purpose flour	300 mL
1 cup	whole wheat flour	250 mL
½ cup	apple butter	125 mL
½ cup	finely chopped walnuts	125 mL

- In a large bowl, cream butter and sugar together until fluffy. Add egg, maple extract, then both flours, working in the last bit by hand, if necessary. Knead dough until smooth and elastic.

- On floured board, roll dough into a rectangle, about 8 x 12 inches (20 x 30 cm).

- Spread apple butter over dough, leaving ½ inch (1 cm) borders. Sprinkle with walnuts and roll from the long side. Wrap in plastic and chill 30 minutes in freezer.

- Preheat oven to 375°F (190°C). Grease and flour a cookie sheet.

- Slice roll into ¼ inch (5 mm) thick slices and arrange flat on cookie sheet. Bake 12 to 15 minutes or until golden. Transfer cookies to wire racks and let cool.

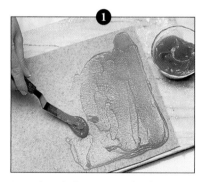

Spread apple butter over dough, leaving ½ inch (1 cm) borders.

Sprinkle with walnuts.

Roll the rectangle from the long side.

SPRITZ COOKIES

(8 dozen)

¾ cup	unsalted butter	175 mL
1 cup	granulated sugar	250 mL
1	egg	1
1 tsp	vanilla extract	5 mL
1¾ cups	all-purpose flour	425 mL
1 cup	confectioners' sugar	250 mL
2-3 tbsp	freshly squeezed lemon juice	30-45 mL

- In a large bowl, cream butter with sugar until light and fluffy. Add egg and vanilla; beat well. Gradually add flour, mixing until well-combined. Chill dough 30 minutes in refrigerator.

- Mix together confectioners' sugar and lemon juice; set icing aside.

- Preheat oven to 375°F (190°C).

- Pack dough into a cookie press and press out different shapes using assorted disks. Arrange on ungreased cookie sheet.

- Bake 8 to 10 minutes until lightly browned. When done, remove from oven and brush with lemon icing. Transfer to wire racks and let cool.

HAZELNUT AND CREAM CHEESE COOKIES
(2 dozen)

½ cup	shortening	125 mL
½ cup	cream cheese, softened	125 mL
½ cup	granulated sugar	125 mL
1 cup	all-purpose flour	250 mL
2 tsp	baking powder	10 mL
1 cup	ground hazelnuts	250 mL
	pinch of salt	

- In a bowl, combine shortening, cream cheese and sugar; mix well. In a separate bowl, mix together flour, baking powder and salt; blend into cream cheese mixture and stir in ½ cup (125 mL) ground hazelnuts.

- Chill dough in refrigerator 1½ to 2 hours.

- Preheat oven to 350°F (180°C). Grease and flour a cookie sheet.

- Shape dough into 1 inch (2.5 cm) balls, coat in remaining ground hazelnuts and place on cookie sheet. Bake 12 minutes and gently transfer to a wire rack; let cool.

93

SWEET BOWS

(3 dozen)

2	eggs	2
1 cup	confectioners' sugar	250 mL
2 tbsp	unsalted butter, melted	30 mL
1 tsp	grated lemon rind	5 mL
1¾ cups	all-purpose flour	425 mL
1 tsp	baking powder	5 mL
	vegetable oil for frying	
	confectioners' sugar	

- In a large bowl, beat eggs and sugar about 5 minutes until light and fluffy. Stir in butter and lemon rind.

- Sift together flour and baking powder; gradually add to egg mixture, blending well after each addition.

- Knead dough on a floured board 3 or 4 times until smooth. Wrap in waxed paper and chill 30 minutes in refrigerator.

- In a deep-fryer or heavy metal pot, heat 4 inches (10 cm) of vegetable oil to 375°F (190°C).

- Divide dough into 2 portions. Keep one chilled and roll the other on a floured board to ⅛ inch (3 mm) thickness. Cut into 1½ x 3 inch (3.5 x 7.5 cm) rectangles. Pinch the center of each rectangle to make bow shapes. Deep-fry until golden, turning once during cooking.

- Remove with slotted spoon and drain on several layers of paper towels; let cool. Store in an airtight container. Sprinkle with confectioners' sugar before serving.

Almond Tuiles
(2 dozen)

1 cup	chopped almonds	250 mL
⅓ cup	granulated sugar	75 mL
1½ tsp	unsalted butter, melted	7 mL
1½ tsp	all-purpose flour	7 mL
2	egg whites	2

- In a bowl, gently mix almonds, sugar, butter and flour with a spatula. Mix in egg whites and chill 1½ hours in refrigerator.

- Preheat oven to 350°F (180°C).

- Drop spoonfuls of batter onto ungreased cookie sheet; spread out with a spatula. Bake 6 to 7 minutes.

- With spatula, gently remove from cookie sheet and wrap around the handle of a wooden spoon to shape into cigarettes. When set, transfer to wire racks and let cool.

PECAN SHORTBREAD MELTS

(3 dozen)

1 cup	unsalted butter, softened	250 mL
⅓ cup	confectioners' sugar	75 mL
2 tsp	vanilla extract	10 mL
2 cups	all-purpose flour	500 mL
¼ tsp	salt	1 mL
¾ cup	finely chopped pecans	175 mL
	superfine sugar	

- Preheat oven to 325°F (160°C).

- Cream butter in large bowl. Blend in confectioners' sugar and vanilla.

- Sift flour and salt into creamed mixture. Blend using wooden spoon. Fold in pecans.

- Shape dough into small balls, the size of dates, and dredge in superfine sugar. Arrange on ungreased cookie sheets.

- Bake 25 to 35 minutes. If desired, broil 2 minutes or until lightly brown.

- When done, transfer to wire racks and let cool.

Cream butter in large bowl. Blend in confectioners' sugar.

Fold in pecans.

Shape dough into small balls, the size of dates.

Dredge in superfine sugar and arrange on ungreased cookie sheets.

Langues de Chat

(3 dozen)

½ cup	unsalted butter, softened	125 mL
⅔ cup	granulated sugar	150 mL
2	eggs, beaten	2
2 tsp	almond extract	10 mL
⅔ cup	all-purpose flour	150 mL

- Preheat oven to 350°F (180°C).

- In a large bowl, cream butter with sugar until light and fluffy. Gradually beat in eggs and almond extract. Sift flour into bowl and fold in gently until smooth.

- Place batter in a pastry bag fitted with a ½ inch (1 cm) plain tip. Pipe 3 inch (7.5 cm) strips onto non-stick cookie sheets, spaced well apart.

- Bake 6 to 8 minutes until golden. Using a spatula, carefully transfer to wire racks and let cool.

CHOCOLATE COOKIES

We all know that there is nothing like chocolate to tantalize the taste buds. Whether you're a chocolate fan or not, you won't be able to resist the delicious cookies in this chapter where chocolate, in all its forms, plays the starring role.

Each recipe includes clear, precise preparation and baking techniques. Follow them closely and the results will speak for themselves!

GLAZED PEANUT BUTTER CHOCOLATE COOKIES

(4 dozen)

½ cup	unsalted butter	125 mL
½ cup	smooth peanut butter	125 mL
½ cup	brown sugar	125 mL
½ cup	granulated sugar	125 mL
1	egg yolk	1
1 tsp	vanilla extract	5 mL
½ cup	whole wheat flour	125 mL
½ cup	all-purpose flour	125 mL
½ cup	crushed corn flakes	125 mL
2 tbsp	cocoa powder	30 mL
½ tsp	baking soda	2 mL

ICING

¼ cup	semi-sweet chocolate chips	50 mL
1 cup	confectioners' sugar	250 mL
3 tbsp	coffee	45 mL

- Preheat oven to 350°F (180°C). Lightly grease cookie sheets.

- In a large bowl, cream butter and peanut butter with both sugars until light and fluffy. Stir in egg yolk and vanilla.

- In another bowl, mix both flours, corn flakes, cocoa and baking soda together; stir into creamed mixture. Turn out onto floured board and knead gently until dough holds together.

- Pull off pieces of dough and shape into 1 inch (2.5 cm) balls. Place on cookie sheet and flatten. Bake 12 to 14 minutes until firm.

- When done, transfer to wire racks and let cool completely before icing.

- To prepare icing, melt chocolate chips over hot water, or in a double-boiler; set aside.

- In a bowl, combine confectioners' sugar and coffee, stirring until sugar is completely dissolved. Blend in melted chocolate. Keep icing soft and spreadable by placing bowl in hot water. Spoon icing generously onto cookies.

ORANGE COOKIES
WITH MELTED CHOCOLATE
(3 dozen)

¼ cup	vegetable shortening	50 mL
½ cup	granulated sugar	125 mL
1	egg	1
2 tbsp	orange zest	30 mL
1 tbsp	orange juice	15 mL
1 cup	all-purpose flour	250 mL
¼ tsp	salt	1 mL
2 tsp	baking powder	10 mL
3	squares sweetened baking chocolate	3
¼ cup	chopped nuts	50 mL

- In a large bowl, cream shortening with sugar. Add egg, orange zest and juice. Sift together flour, salt and baking powder; add to orange batter and mix well. Refrigerate 2 to 3 hours.

- Preheat oven 375°F (190°C). Lightly grease a cookie sheet.

- Roll dough to ¼ inch (5 mm) thickness. Shape cookies with a round cookie cutter about 2⅓ inches (6 cm) in diameter, overlapping circles to make crescents. Transfer to cookie sheet and bake about 10 minutes.

- Meanwhile, melt chocolate in the top of a double-boiler until it is just warm. Dip one end of each cookie in chocolate, then sprinkle with nuts. Let chocolate harden before serving.

CHOCOLATE PEANUT BUTTER AND RAISIN COOKIES

(3 dozen)

½ cup	unsalted butter, at room temperature	125 mL
½ cup	peanut butter	125 mL
1 cup	light brown sugar	250 mL
1	egg, lightly beaten	1
½ tsp	vanilla extract	2 mL
¾ cup	all-purpose flour	175 mL
1 tsp	baking powder	5 mL
⅔ cup	roasted peanuts	150 mL
1 cup	chocolate chips	250 mL
1 cup	sultana raisins	250 mL

- Preheat oven to 375°F (190°C). Grease and flour a cookie sheet.

- In a glass or stainless steel bowl, cream butter and peanut butter. Gradually add brown sugar and mix well to make a smooth batter. Mix in egg and vanilla extract.

- Sift together flour and baking powder; add to batter and blend. Add peanuts, chocolate chips and raisins; mix well. Let stand a few minutes.

- Drop spoonfuls of batter onto cookie sheet, 2 inches (5 cm) apart. Bake cookies about 12 minutes. Let cool before handling.

Cream butter and peanut butter until smooth.

Add sifted flour and baking powder to batter and blend.

Add peanuts, chocolate chips and raisins; mix well.

OATMEAL CHOCOLATE CHIP COOKIES

(4 dozen)

1⅓ cups	unsalted butter, softened	325 mL
1⅓ cups	granulated sugar	325 mL
¾ cup	brown sugar	175 mL
2	eggs	2
1 tsp	vanilla extract	5 mL
2 cups	all-purpose flour	500 mL
1 tsp	baking soda	5 mL
2 cups	oatmeal flakes	500 mL
1½ cups	semi-sweet chocolate chips	375 mL
½ cup	finely chopped walnuts	125 mL
	pinch of salt	

- Preheat oven to 375°F (190°C). Lightly grease a cookie sheet.

- In large bowl, cream butter with both sugars until fluffy. Beat in eggs and vanilla.

- Sift flour with baking soda and salt. Stir into batter. Add oats, chocolate chips and walnuts, mixing well after each addition.

- Drop small spoonfuls of batter onto cookie sheet and bake about 10 minutes. When done, carefully transfer cookies to wire racks and let cool.

*C*HOCOLATE WALNUT COOKIES

(4 dozen)

½ cup	shortening	125 mL
1⅔ cups	granulated sugar	400 mL
2	eggs, beaten	2
1 tsp	vanilla extract	5 mL
2	squares semi-sweet baking chocolate, melted	2
2 cups	all-purpose flour	500 mL
¼ tsp	salt	1 mL
½ tsp	baking soda	2 mL
1 tsp	baking powder	5 mL
⅓ cup	heavy cream	75 mL
⅔ cup	chopped walnuts	150 mL
	confectioners' sugar	

- Preheat oven to 350°F (180°C). Grease and flour a cookie sheet.

- Cream shortening with sugar in bowl. Beat in eggs, vanilla and melted chocolate.

- Sift flour with salt, baking soda and baking powder. Add half to chocolate mixture, mixing well. Add half of cream and blend thoroughly.

- Add remaining flour and cream to batter and mix well. If batter is too stiff, add a little more cream. Stir in walnuts and chill 1 hour in refrigerator.

- Shape dough into small balls and dust with confectioners' sugar. Arrange balls on cookie sheet and bake about 12 minutes or according to size.

- When done, carefully transfer cookies to wire rack and let cool.

CHOCOLATE ROLLUPS

(32 rollups)

¾ cup	unsalted butter	175 mL
¾ cup	granulated sugar	175 mL
1	egg	1
½ tsp	maple extract	2 mL
1 ¼ cups	all-purpose flour	300 mL
¾ cup	whole wheat flour	175 mL
½ cup	chocolate hazelnut spread	125 mL
½ cup	finely chopped hazelnuts	125 mL

- Preheat oven to 375°F (190°C); grease and flour a cookie sheet.

- In a large bowl, cream butter with sugar until fluffy. Add egg and maple extract. Add both flours, working in last bit by hand, if necessary.

- Soften chocolate hazelnut spread over hot water or in microwave.

- Divide dough into 4 portions. On floured board, roll one portion into a circle, 8 inches (20 cm) in diameter. Keep remaining portions refrigerated.

- Spread 2 tbsp (30 mL) of chocolate hazelnut spread over circle and sprinkle with 2 tbsp (30 mL) of nuts. Cut into 8 wedges and roll each one up, starting at wide edge. Repeat with remaining portions of dough, spread and nuts.

- Arrange rollups on cookie sheet and bake 12 to 15 minutes until golden. When done, transfer to wire racks and let cool.

CHOCOLATE SANDWICHES
(2½ dozen)

⅓ cup	vegetable shortening	75 mL
¾ cup	granulated sugar	175 mL
1	egg	1
1 tbsp	orange juice concentrate	15 mL
1¼ cups	all-purpose flour	300 mL
⅓ cup	cocoa powder	75 mL
1 cup	confectioners' sugar	250 mL
1 tbsp	vegetable shortening	15 mL
2-3 tsp	milk	10-15 mL

- Preheat oven to 375°F (190°C).

- In a large bowl, cream shortening with sugar. Add egg and orange juice concentrate; beat well.

- Mix flour and cocoa. Gradually add to egg mixture, kneading in the last bit until dough is smooth.

- Working with half the dough at a time, roll out on floured board as thinly as possible. Cut into circles, about 2 inches (5 cm) in diameter, and bake 8 to 10 minutes on ungreased cookie sheets, until cookies begin to harden. When done, transfer to wire racks and let cool.

- To prepare filling, blend 1 tbsp (15 mL) of shortening into confectioners' sugar. Add enough milk to obtain desired consistency.

- When cookies are completely cool, spread filling onto bottoms of half the cookies. Top each one with another cookie to make a sandwich.

CHOCO-BANANA DROPS
(2 dozen)

⅓ cup	mashed banana	75 mL
1 tbsp	melted unsalted butter	15 mL
2 tbsp	brown sugar	30 mL
1 tbsp	corn syrup	15 mL
⅓ cup	sweetened condensed milk	75 mL
1 cup	crushed corn flakes	250 mL
½ cup	all-purpose flour	125 mL
½ tsp	baking soda	2 mL
⅓ cup	butterscotch chips	75 mL
⅓ cup	chocolate chips	75 mL
¼ cup	chopped walnuts	50 mL

- Heat oven to 350°F (180°C); grease and flour a cookie sheet.

- In a bowl, combine banana and butter. Blend in brown sugar, corn syrup, condensed milk, then corn flakes.

- Sift flour with baking soda. Mix into batter. Stir in butterscotch chips, chocolate chips and walnuts.

- Drop spoonfuls of batter onto cookie sheet. Bake 10 to 12 minutes, or until firm. When done, transfer cookies to wire rack and let cool.

$\mathcal{N}$O-BAKE CHOCOLATE BALLS

(2½ dozen)

½ cup	peanut butter chips	125 mL
¼ cup	unsalted butter	50 mL
1 cup	confectioners' sugar	250 mL
½ cup	chopped dates	125 mL
½ cup	chopped walnuts	125 mL
¼ cup	white chocolate chips	50 mL
2 tbsp	orange juice	30 mL
1 tsp	grated orange rind	5 mL
2 cups	crispy rice cereal	500 mL
6	squares semi-sweet baking chocolate	6

- Melt peanut butter chips and butter in a pan over hot water. Set aside to cool.

- In a large bowl, combine confectioners' sugar, dates, walnuts and white chocolate chips, mixing thoroughly so that all pieces of date are separated and coated with sugar.

- Add orange juice and rind to butter mixture; blend into date mixture. Fold in cereal.

- With wet hands, shape dough into 1 inch (2.5 cm) balls. Chill in refrigerator.

- Melt baking chocolate over hot water, or in a double-boiler. Dip chilled balls in chocolate and set aside on waxed paper to let chocolate harden before serving.

CHUNKY CHOCOLATE CHIP COOKIES

(3 dozen)

1 cup	unsalted butter	250 mL
¾ cup	brown sugar	175 mL
¾ cup	granulated sugar	175 mL
2	eggs	2
2 cups	all-purpose flour	500 mL
½ tsp	salt	2 mL
1 tsp	baking soda	5 mL
¾ cup	chocolate chips	175 mL
4	squares semi-sweet baking chocolate, in chunks	4
¼ tsp	almond extract	1 mL

- Preheat oven to 375°F (190°C). Grease and flour a cookie sheet.

- In large bowl, cream butter with both sugars until light and fluffy. Add eggs and continue beating 1 minute.

- Combine dry ingredients and gradually add to batter, beating at low speed. Mix in chocolate chips, chocolate chunks and almond extract.

- Drop small spoonfuls of batter onto cookie sheet and bake 10 minutes. When done, carefully transfer cookies to wire racks and let cool.

113

CHOCOLATE ORANGE COOKIES

(3 dozen)

½ cup	vegetable shortening	125 mL
1 cup	granulated sugar	250 mL
2	eggs, beaten	2
2 tsp	grated orange zest	10 mL
2 cups	all-purpose flour	500 mL
⅓ cup	cocoa powder	75 mL
1 tsp	baking powder	5 mL
3 tbsp	orange juice	45 mL

- In a large bowl, cream shortening with sugar. Add eggs and orange zest; mix well.

- Sift together flour, cocoa and baking powder. Gradually stir dry ingredients into egg mixture, alternating with orange juice and ending with dry ingredients.

- Wrap dough in plastic and chill in refrigerator 3 hours.

- Preheat oven to 400°F (200°C). Grease and flour a cookie sheet.

- Roll dough to ¼ inch (5 mm) thickness and shape into cookies with assorted cookie cutters. Arrange on cookie sheet and bake 8 to 10 minutes. Decorate with icing, if desired.

CHOCOLATE PARTY COOKIES
(2 dozen)

½ cup	unsalted butter, softened	125 mL
½ cup	brown sugar	125 mL
1 tsp	vanilla extract	5 mL
1	egg	1
1 cup	all-purpose flour	250 mL
¼ tsp	baking soda	1 mL
½ tsp	salt	2 mL
1 cup	chocolate chips	250 mL
	choice of garnish	

- Preheat oven to 350°F (180°C). Grease and flour a cookie sheet.

- With an electric beater, mix together butter and brown sugar. Add vanilla extract and egg; continue beating 5 minutes.

- Sift together flour, baking soda and salt; delicately stir dry ingredients into butter mixture to make a smooth batter. Fold in chocolate chips, or if desired, leave cookies plain and use chocolate chips as garnish.

- With your hands, shape dough into small flat rounds, place on cookie sheet and decorate with the garnish of your choice.

- Bake about 10 minutes. Let cool before serving.

CHOCOLATE CHECKERBOARDS
(4 dozen)

1	square unsweetened baking chocolate	1
½ cup	butter	125 mL
½ cup	vegetable shortening	125 mL
1 cup	granulated sugar	250 mL
1	egg	1
1 tbsp	Amaretto liqueur	15 mL
2 cups	all-purpose flour	500 mL
1	egg white	1

- Melt chocolate over hot water. Set aside to cool.

- In a large bowl, cream butter and shortening with sugar until light and fluffy. Add egg and liqueur; blend well.

- Mix in flour, working the last bit in by hand, if necessary. Knead dough on floured board until smooth.

- Divide dough in half. To one portion, add melted chocolate. Wrap both portions separately in waxed paper and chill about 2 hours in refrigerator.

- Divide each portion in half and roll each half into a long rope about 1 inch (2.5 cm) in diameter and 12 inches (30 cm) long. Brush each rope with lightly beaten egg white.

- Press together one dark rope and one light rope. Stack another pair of ropes on top, alternating colors. Wrap in waxed paper, pressing it into a square log as you wrap. Chill for at least 2 hours.

- Preheat oven to 375°F (190°C). Cut dough into ¼ inch (5 mm) thick slices. Bake 8 to 10 minutes on ungreased cookie sheet, until edges begin to brown. Transfer to wire racks and let cool.

Divide each portion in half and roll each half into a long rope about 1 inch (2.5 cm) in diameter and 12 inches (30 cm) long.

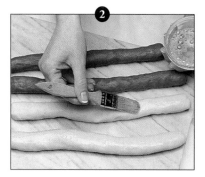

Brush each rope with lightly beaten egg white.

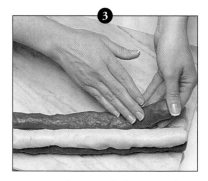

Press together one dark rope and one light rope. Stack another pair of ropes on top, alternating colors, to make a square log.

DOUBLE CHOCOLATE CHUNK COOKIES WITH PECANS

(3 dozen)

1 cup	unsalted butter, softened	250 mL
1 cup	granulated sugar	250 mL
½ cup	brown sugar	125 mL
2	large eggs	2
1 tsp	vanilla extract	5 mL
2⅓ cups	all-purpose flour	575 mL
1 tsp	baking soda	5 mL
6	squares white baking chocolate, in chunks	6
6	squares bittersweet baking chocolate, in chunks	6
½ cup	chopped pecans	125 mL

- Preheat oven to 375°F (190°C). Grease a cookie sheet.

- In large bowl, cream butter with both sugars. Beat in eggs and vanilla, mixing until light and fluffy.

- Sift dry ingredients together and stir into batter. Fold in chocolate chunks and pecans.

- Drop small spoonfuls of batter onto cookie sheet. Bake 10 to 12 minutes or until edges are lightly browned.

- When done, carefully transfer cookies to wire racks and let cool.

PEANUT BUTTER COOKIES WITH DOUBLE CHOCOLATE CHIPS

(3 dozen)

½ cup	shortening	125 mL
¼ cup	granulated sugar	50 mL
½ cup	brown sugar	125 mL
1	egg	1
½ cup	crunchy peanut butter	125 mL
1 ½ cups	all-purpose flour	375 mL
1 tsp	baking soda	5 mL
½ cup	semi-sweet chocolate chips	125 mL
½ cup	white chocolate chips	125 mL
	pinch of salt	

- Preheat oven to 375°F (190°C).

- Cream shortening with both sugars in large bowl. Beat in egg and then peanut butter.

- Sift flour with baking soda and salt. Add to batter, mixing just enough to combine. Stir in chocolate chips.

- Shape dough into small balls and arrange on ungreased cookie sheet. Flatten with fork and bake 8 to 10 minutes.

- When done, carefully transfer cookies to wire racks and let cool.

WHITE CHOCOLATE AND BUTTERSCOTCH COOKIES

(3½ dozen)

½ cup	unsalted butter, softened	125 mL
¾ cup	granulated sugar	175 mL
2	eggs	2
3 tbsp	light cream	45 mL
2 cups	all-purpose flour	500 mL
½ tsp	baking soda	2 mL
½ cup	cocoa powder	125 mL
½ cup	white chocolate chips	125 mL
½ cup	butterscotch chips	125 mL
	pinch of salt	

- Preheat oven to 350°F (180°C). Grease a cookie sheet.

- In large bowl, cream butter with sugar and beat 3 minutes. Add eggs and continue beating until fluffy. Beat in cream.

- Sift dry ingredients together over batter and mix well. Fold in chocolate and butterscotch chips.

- Drop small spoonfuls of batter onto cookie sheet and bake 8 to 10 minutes. When done, carefully transfer cookies to wire racks and let cool.

GINGERED CHOCOLATE FINGERS

(2 dozen)

14 oz	marzipan	400 g
½ cup	crystallized ginger, finely chopped	125 mL
9	squares semi-sweet baking chocolate, melted	9
1 tbsp	vegetable oil	15 mL
	cocoa powder	

• In a bowl, knead marzipan and ginger until well-combined. Pinch off small pieces and shape into fingers, about 2½ inches (6 cm) long.

• Mix melted chocolate with oil. Dip fingers in chocolate mixture. Place on a wire rack and chill in refrigerator until chocolate hardens. Sprinkle with cocoa.

CHOCOLATE CHIP COOKIES
(2 dozen)

1 ½ tbsp	unsalted butter, softened	25 mL
⅓ cup	vegetable shortening, softened	75 mL
¼ cup	brown sugar	50 mL
⅓ cup	granulated sugar	75 mL
1 cup	cake flour	250 mL
1 tsp	baking powder	5 mL
¼ tsp	salt	1 mL
1	small egg	1
½ cup	chocolate chips	125 mL

- Preheat oven to 375°F (190°C). Grease and flour a cookie sheet.

- In a large bowl, mix together butter, shortening and both sugars. Sift together flour, baking powder and salt. With the tips of your fingers, work the dry ingredients into the butter mixture. Add egg and chocolate chips; mix well to obtain a stiff dough.

- With a pastry bag fitted with a large round tube, squeeze dough out onto cookie sheet.* Bake cookies until golden.

*NOTE: *dough can be spooned onto cookie sheet as well, although appearance will be more like a drop cookie when baked.*

*C*HOCOLATE-FROSTED
MARSHMALLOW COOKIES
(2 dozen)

½ cup	unsalted butter	125 mL
1 cup	brown sugar	250 mL
1	egg	1
½ cup	milk	125 mL
1 tsp	vanilla extract	5 mL
1½ cups	all-purpose flour	375 mL
½ tsp	baking soda	2 mL
12	large marshmallows, halved crosswise	12

ICING

3	squares semi-sweet baking chocolate	3
¼ cup	unsalted butter	50 mL

⊚

- Preheat oven to 350°F (180°C). Lightly grease a cookie sheet.

- In a large bowl, cream butter with brown sugar. Add egg, milk and vanilla, and continue beating until light and fluffy. Stir in flour and baking soda.

- On a lightly floured board, roll dough ¼ inch (5 mm) thick. Shape cookies with a 1½ inch (4 cm) round cookie cutter. Arrange on cookie sheet and bake 6 minutes.

- Remove from oven and immediately place half a marshmallow, cut-side-down, on each cookie. Return to oven and bake 2 more minutes until marshmallow sticks to cookie. Transfer to wire racks and let cool.

- Prepare icing: in a small heavy saucepan over low heat, melt chocolate and butter; stir to blend. Spoon frosting over cookies, covering marshmallows.

CHOCOLATE PRETZELS
(3 dozen)

2	squares unsweetened baking chocolate	2
¼ cup	unsalted butter, softened	50 mL
¼ cup	vegetable shortening	50 mL
½ cup	brown sugar	125 mL
½ tsp	cinnamon	2 mL
2	eggs	2
2¼ cups	all-purpose flour	550 mL
1	egg white, lightly beaten	1
	pinch of salt	
	coarse sugar	

- Melt chocolate over hot water; set aside to cool.

- In a medium bowl, cream butter and shortening with brown sugar. Stir in cinnamon, eggs and melted chocolate.

- Sift flour and salt into chocolate batter and mix, first with a wooden spoon, then with your hands, to make a smooth dough. Wrap dough in plastic and chill 1 hour in refrigerator.

- Preheat oven to 350°F (180°C). Grease a cookie sheet.

- Shape dough into walnut-size balls. Roll each into a thin strand, about 10 inches (25 cm) long. Bring ends together to form a loop, crossing ends over. Take ends back up to top of loop and press together to seal.

- Arrange on cookie sheet, brush with egg white and sprinkle with coarse sugar. Bake 12 to 15 minutes. Transfer to wire racks and let cool.

BROWNIE DROP COOKIES
WITH MACADAMIA NUTS
(2 dozen)

6	squares milk chocolate baking chocolate	6
2 tbsp	unsalted butter	30 mL
2	eggs	2
¼ tsp	vanilla extract	1 mL
1 cup	granulated sugar	250 mL
⅓ cup	all-purpose flour	75 mL
½ tsp	baking powder	2 mL
¾ cup	chopped macadamia nuts	175 mL
	pinch of salt	

- Preheat oven to 350°F (180°C). Lightly grease and flour a cookie sheet.

- Melt chocolate and butter slowly in top of double-boiler. Remove from heat and let cool slightly.

- In large bowl, beat eggs until light and pale. Add vanilla and sugar; beat until very thick. Mix in melted chocolate.

- Sift flour with baking powder and salt. Blend into batter and stir in nuts.

- Drop small spoonfuls of batter onto cookie sheet and bake about 10 minutes. When done, carefully transfer cookies to wire racks and let cool.

Melt chocolate and butter slowly in top of double-boiler.

Add vanilla and sugar to beaten eggs.

Mix in melted chocolate.

Blend in sifted flour, baking powder and salt. Stir in nuts.

CHOCOLATE CHIP CARAMEL COOKIES
(3 dozen)

½ cup	unsalted butter	125 mL
½ cup	brown sugar	125 mL
¾ cup	granulated sugar	175 mL
1	large egg, beaten	1
2 tbsp	heavy cream	30 mL
1½ cups	all-purpose flour	375 mL
¼ tsp	salt	1 mL
½ cup	semi-sweet chocolate chips	125 mL
½ cup	slivered almonds	125 mL
12	caramels,* cut in half	12

- Preheat oven to 375°F (190°C). Lightly grease and flour a cookie sheet.

- In a large bowl, cream butter with both sugars until light and fluffy. Add egg and continue beating 1 minute. Beat in cream.

- Combine dry ingredients and add to batter, beating at low speed. Mix in chocolate chips, almonds and caramels.

- Drop small spoonfuls of batter onto cookie sheet and bake 8 minutes. When done, carefully transfer cookies to wire rack and let cool.

*NOTE: *if possible, caramels should be the hard variety.*

FILLED AND GARNISHED COOKIES

Filled and garnished cookies are always a big hit and they are a lot less compli-
cated to prepare than you might think. A wonderful variety of fillings allows you
to blend flavors and textures to your heart's content. Some cookies are best filled
and garnished before baking, and others only when they are done–in which case
it is best to first let the cookies cool completely so that the filling doesn't melt.

With their delicious surprises inside, these crisp cookies are sure to become everyone's favorite.

129

CREAM HORNS
(2 dozen)

½ cup	all-purpose flour	125 mL
½ cup	granulated sugar	125 mL
¼ cup	finely ground almonds	50 mL
2	egg whites	2
4 tbsp	melted unsalted butter	60 mL
1 tsp	orange rind	5 mL
1 cup	chestnut purée	250 mL
1 tbsp	Amaretto liqueur	15 mL
1 tsp	almond extract	5 mL
1 cup	whipping cream, whipped	250 mL

- Preheat oven to 325°F (160°C); grease and flour a cookie sheet.

- Combine flour, sugar and almonds in a large bowl. Beat egg whites and gradually stir into almond mixture along with melted butter and orange rind.

- Drop 6 large spoonfuls of batter onto a cookie sheet. With a wet fork, spread batter as thinly as possible into large circles. Bake 10 to 12 minutes, until firm and just turning golden at the edges.

- Gently mold each cookie around a metal horn, and bake the next batch. When done, remove first batch of cookies from horn molds and mold the second batch. Repeat with remaining batter. Keep horns in airtight container until ready to fill with chestnut cream.

- To prepare filling, soften chestnut purée; blend in liqueur and almond extract. Fold purée into whipped cream.

- Spoon chestnut cream into pastry bag and fill each horn with about 1½ tbsp (25 mL) of filling. Serve immediately.

ease 2 baki...
...t gas 4. Mix
almonds and s...
In a mixi...
butter until l...
and beat until ...fluffy.
Beat in the egg yolk. Fold in the
flour mixture first using a knife
and then the fingers. Knead the
dough on a floured surface.
Cut with a 2 1/2" cutter.

BUCKWHEAT COOKIES

(3 dozen)

1 cup	unsalted butter	250 mL
½ cup	granulated sugar	125 mL
2	eggs, beaten	2
¾ tsp	vanilla extract	4 mL
½ cup	molasses	125 mL
3½ cups	buckwheat flour	875 mL
2 tsp	baking soda	10 mL
1½ tbsp	granulated sugar	25 mL
½ cup	strawberry jam	125 mL
	pinch of salt	

- In a large bowl, cream together butter and sugar. Beating constantly, gradually add eggs, vanilla and molasses. Mix together buckwheat flour, baking soda and salt; add to egg mixture. Cover dough and chill 2 hours in refrigerator.

- Preheat oven to 350°F (180°C). Grease a cookie sheet.

- On a floured board, roll dough ⅛ inch (3 mm) thick. Shape cookies with a 2 inch (5 cm) round cookie cutter. With a smaller cookie cutter, make a hole in the center of half the cookies. Cover each whole cookie with one that has a hole. Transfer to cookie sheet and sprinkle with sugar.

- Bake 10 to 12 minutes and let cool. Garnish each with 1 tbsp (15 mL) of jam.

APPLE AND CINNAMON SANDWICH COOKIES

(2 dozen)

3	apples, peeled, cored and diced	3
2 tbsp	apple jelly	30 mL
1 tbsp	honey	15 mL
½ tsp	cinnamon	2 mL
¾ cup	granulated sugar	175 mL
½ cup	unsalted butter, softened	125 mL
½ cup	vegetable shortening	125 mL
½ tsp	vanilla extract	2 mL
1	egg	1
2 cups	all-purpose flour	500 mL
1 tsp	baking powder	5 mL

- In a small saucepan over medium heat, cook apples, apple jelly, honey and cinnamon 10 minutes. Let cool and set aside.

- In a large bowl, mix together sugar, butter, shortening, vanilla and egg. Stir in flour and baking powder. Cover and chill 1 hour in refrigerator.

- Preheat oven to 350°F (180°C). Grease a cookie sheet.

- Divide dough in half and roll each portion separately on lightly floured board into a rectangle, about 9 x 12 inches (23 x 30 cm). Cut into 1¼ x 2¼ inch (3 x 6 cm) rectangles.

- Drop 1 tbsp (15 mL) of apple filling on half of rectangles, then cover with another rectangle. Press edges together to seal. Make 2 small incisions on the top of each sandwich. Arrange on cookie sheet and bake about 10 minutes. Transfer to wire racks and let cool.

DATE SANDWICH COOKIES
(2 dozen)

1 cup	unsalted butter	250 mL
¾ cup	brown sugar	175 mL
1	egg	1
⅓ cup	molasses	75 mL
1 tsp	vanilla extract	5 mL
¼ cup	boiling water	50 mL
4 cups	all-purpose flour	1 L
2 tsp	baking soda	10 mL
2 cups	chopped dates	500 mL
½ cup	boiling water	125 mL
¼ cup	granulated sugar	50 mL
	pinch of salt	
	sugar	

- Preheat oven to 325°F (160°C). Grease a cookie sheet.

- In a large bowl, cream together butter and brown sugar. In another bowl, beat egg with molasses, vanilla, and then ¼ cup (50 mL) of boiling water. Stir this mixture into the first.

- Sift together flour and baking soda and add to batter; mix well.

- Roll dough out about ¼ inch (5 mm) thick. Shape cookies with a cookie cutter.

- In a saucepan, combine dates, ½ cup (125 mL) boiling water and granulated sugar. Bring to a boil and let simmer 3 minutes; let cool slightly.

- Top half of cookies with date mixture and cover with remaining cookies. Sprinkle with sugar. Transfer to cookie sheet and bake 12 to 15 minutes. Let cool on wire racks.

Roll dough out about ¼ inch (5 mm) thick. Shape cookies with a cookie cutter.

Top half of cookies with date mixture.

Cover with remaining cookies.

CHOCOLATE CARAMEL SANDWICHES

(3 dozen)

¾ cup	unsalted butter	175 mL
1 cup	confectioners' sugar	250 mL
2	eggs	2
4 tbsp	orange juice	60 mL
½ cup	all-purpose flour	125 mL
½ cup	corn flour	125 mL
⅓ cup	cocoa powder	75 mL

CARAMEL FILLING

3½ oz	caramels (about 13)	100 g
1 tbsp	unsalted butter	15 mL
2 tbsp	sweetened condensed milk	30 mL

- Preheat oven to 350°F (180°C); lightly grease cookie sheets.

- In a large bowl, cream butter with confectioners' sugar until fluffy. Blend in eggs and orange juice.

- Sift together all-purpose flour, corn flour and cocoa. Gradually blend into creamed mixture.

- Spoon mixture into pastry bag with a fluted tube. Pipe 1 x 3 inch (2.5 x 7.5 cm) strips, 2 inches (5 cm) apart, onto cookie sheets.

- Bake 8 to 10 minutes, until just beginning to shrink at the edges. Transfer to wire racks and let cool.

- To prepare filling, combine caramels, butter and condensed milk in small saucepan. Place over very low heat, stirring constantly, until melted and smooth.

- Spread filling on bottom side of half the cookies. Place another cookie on top, bottom side to filling, pressing slightly to make sandwiches. (If filling begins to harden, set container over a bowl of hot water.)

- Chill for a few minutes in refrigerator until filling hardens.

PEANUT BUTTER SANDWICH COOKIES

(3 dozen)

½ cup	vegetable shortening	125 mL
1¼ cups	brown sugar	300 mL
3	eggs, beaten	3
1 tsp	vanilla extract	5 mL
5 cups	all-purpose flour	1.25 L
1 tbsp	baking powder	15 mL
¼ tsp	salt	1 mL
¼ cup	milk	50 mL
½ cup	granulated sugar	125 mL
½ cup	currants	125 mL
½ cup	peanut butter	125 mL

- Preheat oven to 350°F (180°C). Grease a cookie sheet.

- In a large bowl, cream together shortening and brown sugar. Add eggs and vanilla extract; mix well.

- Sift together flour, baking powder and salt, and gradually add to egg mixture, alternating with milk. Chill 10 minutes in refrigerator.

- Roll out dough to ⅛ inch (3 mm) thickness. Shape with a 3 inch (8 cm) round cookie cutter. Prick tops of cookies with a fork, transfer to cookie sheet and bake 10 minutes.

- Meanwhile, in a saucepan, bring sugar, 1 tsp (5 mL) flour, currants and ½ cup (125 mL) water to a boil; cook until mixture thickens. Remove from heat and stir in peanut butter.

- Spread 2 tsp (10 mL) of peanut butter mixture over half of cookies. Cover each with another cookie and serve.

Almond Wafers
WITH RED CURRANT JELLY
(4 dozen)

¾ cup	**ground blanched almonds**	175 mL
2 cups	**all-purpose flour**	500 mL
¾ cup	**unsalted butter**	175 mL
6 tbsp	**granulated sugar**	90 mL
1	**egg**	1
½ cup	**white icing**	125 mL
¼ cup	**red currant jelly**	50 mL
	pinch of salt	

- Combine almonds and flour in a large bowl. Make a well in the center and add remaining ingredients, except icing and jelly.

- Using tips of fingers, blend ingredients to form dough. Knead until smooth and shape into a ball. Wrap in a clean cloth and chill 1 hour in refrigerator.

- Preheat oven to 375°F (190°C).

- On lightly floured surface, roll dough into a rectangle about ⅛ inch (3 mm) thick. Trim edges and cut into 2 inch (5 cm) squares.

- Arrange on cookie sheet and bake 8 minutes. Carefully transfer to wire rack and let cool.

- Decorate half of cookies with icing piped through a fine tube. On remaining cookies, spread red currant jelly, top with iced cookies and serve.

COFFEE-CREAM ROLLUPS
(3 dozen)

½ cup	brown sugar	125 mL
½ cup	corn syrup	125 mL
⅓ cup	unsalted butter	75 mL
3 tbsp	flaked coconut	45 mL
1 cup	all-purpose flour	250 mL
½ tsp	baking powder	2 mL
1 tbsp	coffee-flavored liqueur	15 mL

FILLING

1 cup	whipping cream	250 mL
1 tbsp	coffee-flavored liqueur	15 mL

- Preheat oven to 325°F (160°C).

- In a small saucepan over low heat, combine brown sugar, syrup and butter. Stir until sugar is dissolved. Transfer to a large bowl and add coconut.

- Sift flour with baking powder and add to mixture along with liqueur; mix well.

- Drop spoonfuls of batter onto ungreased cookie sheet, only 6 at a time. Bake 7 to 9 minutes, until batter spreads and bubbles form on the surface.

- Remove from oven and let stand on cookie sheet about 1 minute. Roll 3 at a time around the handle of a wooden spoon. If cookies become too hard to remove from cookie sheet, return to oven for about 30 seconds.

- Slip rollups off wooden spoon and let cool on wire racks. Store in an airtight container.

- When ready to serve, whip cream and add liqueur. Pipe about 1½ tsp (7 mL) into the end of each rollup.

Apricot Newtons
(1½ dozen)

½ cup	unsalted butter	125 mL
4 oz	cream cheese	125 g
¾ cup	granulated sugar	175 mL
2 cups	all-purpose flour	500 mL
½ tsp	baking powder	2 mL
1 cup	dried apricots	250 mL
3 tbsp	corn syrup	45 mL

- In a large bowl, cream butter and cream cheese with sugar. Sift flour with baking powder and add to creamed mixture. Chill dough for 4 hours or until firm.

- While dough is chilling, prepare filling: in a saucepan, cover apricots with water and simmer until fruit is soft. Purée apricots, add corn syrup and continue cooking until it thickens into a jam; let cool.

- Preheat oven to 350°F (180°C); grease and flour a cookie sheet.

- Divide dough into 3 portions. While rolling one portion, keep remainder chilled. Roll dough on floured board into a 6 x 10 inch (15 x 25 cm) rectangle. Spread ⅓ of filling down length of rectangle, just to the left of center. Using a pastry brush, moisten ½ inch (1 cm) of right edge with water.

- Lift left edge of dough over filling. Lift right edge to overlap dough. Press gently to seal. Pinch ends closed. Repeat with remaining dough and filling.

- Using a broad spatula, transfer to cookie sheet, seam side down. Bake 20 to 25 minutes, until golden.

- Let cool for 5 minutes on cookie sheet, then trim irregular ends. Cut into 1½ inch (4 cm) bars. Transfer to wire rack to cool completely.

FIG DEMILUNES
(1½ dozen)

¾ cup	butter	175 mL
1 cup	granulated sugar	250 mL
1	egg	1
¼ tsp	almond extract	1 mL
1¾ cups	all-purpose flour	425 mL
1	egg yolk	1
1 tsp	water	5 mL
FILLING		
12	dried figs, stems discarded	12
2 tsp	honey	10 mL

- In a large bowl, cream butter with sugar. Add egg and almond extract, and beat until well-blended. Gradually fold in flour, working dough by hand until smooth.

- Refrigerate for 30 minutes.

- Place figs in a saucepan. Cover with water and cook until soft, about 15 minutes. Drain, reserving cooking liquid. Purée figs; mix in honey and ¼ cup (50 mL) cooking liquid to make a thick paste. Let cool.

- Preheat oven to 350°F (180°C); lightly grease cookie sheets.

- On well-floured board, roll dough out about ½ inch (5 mm) thick and cut into circles, 3 inches (7.5 cm) in diameter.

- Place heaping teaspoonful (about 7 mL) of filling to one side on each circle.

- With pastry brush and water, wet edge of other side of circle. Fold over to form semi-circle. Crimp edges with a fork.

- Mix egg yolk with 1 tsp (5 mL) water, and brush onto demilunes. Bake 20 to 25 minutes until golden. Transfer to wire racks and let cool.

HAMENTASHEN
(3 dozen)

FILLING

12 oz	pitted prunes	350 g
½ cup	finely chopped almonds	125 mL
1 tbsp	grated orange rind	15 mL

PASTRY

1 cup	vegetable shortening	250 mL
2	eggs	2
1 cup	honey	250 mL
4 cups	all-purpose flour	1 L
1 tsp	baking powder	5 mL

- Place prunes in a saucepan with just enough water to cover them. Cook until soft and drain, reserving cooking liquid.

- Purée prunes, adding only enough cooking liquid to make about 2 cups (500 mL) of thick paste. Stir in almonds and orange rind.

- Preheat oven to 350°F (180°C); lightly grease cookie sheets.

- To prepare pastry, cream shortening in a large bowl; mix in eggs and honey.

- Sift flour and baking powder together. Add to egg mixture, working last of flour in by hand, if necessary.

- On floured board, roll dough out ¼ inch (5 mm) thick. Cut into 3 inch (7.5 cm) rounds. Place a large spoonful of filling in center of each round. Draw edges together to form triangle and pinch seams to seal.

- Bake 16 minutes until golden. Transfer to wire racks and let cool.

VARIATION: *Poppy Seed Filling. Grind 2 cups (500 mL) poppy seeds in blender. Transfer to a saucepan; combine with ¾ cup (175 mL) raisins, and ½ cup (125 mL) honey. Add 1 tsp (5 mL) grated lemon rind. Cook over low heat, stirring until mixture becomes a thick paste. Cool before using.*

RASPBERRY OATMEAL TURNOVERS

(2 dozen)

⅓ cup	unsalted butter	75 mL
½ cup	vegetable shortening	125 mL
1 cup	brown sugar	250 mL
1	egg	1
1	egg yolk	1
1¾ cups	all-purpose flour	425 mL
1 cup	oatmeal flakes	250 mL
½ cup	finely shredded coconut	125 mL
½ tsp	baking soda	2 mL
1½ tsp	baking powder	7 mL
⅔ cup	raspberry jam	150 mL
	pinch of salt	

• Preheat oven to 325°F (160°C). Grease and flour a cookie sheet.

• In a bowl, cream together butter, shortening and brown sugar. Add egg and egg yolk and then dry ingredients, beating at low speed after each addition, to make a lumpy dough.

• On a floured board, roll dough out thinly and cut into 4 inch (10 cm) squares. Drop a large spoonful of raspberry jam into the center of each square, brush edges with a bit of water then fold dough over to make a triangle; press edges together to seal. Make 3 small incisions in the top of each turnover.

• Transfer to cookie sheet and bake about 15 minutes, or until lightly golden. Let cool.

Cut dough into 4 inch (10 cm) squares. Drop a large spoonful of raspberry jam into the center of each square.

Brush edges with a bit of water.

Fold dough over to make a triangle; press edges together to seal.

CHESTNUT SANDWICH COOKIES

(2½ dozen)

1 cup	butter, softened	250 mL
1 cup	granulated sugar	250 mL
1 tsp	vanilla extract	5 mL
2 tbsp	orange liqueur	30 mL
3	large egg whites	3
2 cups	ground almonds	500 mL
½ cup	all-purpose flour	125 mL
¾ cup	chestnut purée	175 mL

- Preheat oven to 350°F (180°C). Grease and flour a cookie sheet.

- In large bowl, cream butter with sugar until fluffy. Beat in vanilla, liqueur and egg whites, one at a time, beating well between additions. Gently fold in ground almonds and flour.

- Spoon mixture into pastry bag fitted with ½ inch (1 cm) plain tip. Pipe dough onto prepared cookie sheet in small rounds. Bake cookies 12 to 14 minutes.

- When cookies are done, carefully transfer to wire rack and let cool. Spread chestnut purée over half of cookies and top with remaining cookies to make sandwiches.

CHOCOLATE RAVIOLI COOKIES

(3 dozen)

4	squares semi-sweet chocolate	4
½ cup	unsalted butter, softened	125 mL
¼ cup	vegetable shortening	50 mL
¾ cup	granulated sugar	175 mL
2	eggs	2
2¼ cups	all-purpose flour	550 mL
½ tsp	baking powder	2 mL
¼ tsp	salt	1 mL
¼ tsp	baking soda	1 mL
½ cup	ricotta cheese	125 mL
3 tbsp	chopped hazelnuts	45 mL

- Melt 2 squares of chocolate in the top of a double-boiler; let cool.

- In a large bowl, mix together butter, shortening, sugar and eggs. Stir in melted chocolate. Add flour, baking powder, salt and baking soda; mix well. Cover and refrigerate 1 hour, or until dough is firm.

- To make filling, melt remaining chocolate. Add ricotta cheese and hazelnuts; mix well and set filling aside.

- Preheat oven to 350°F (180°C).

- On a floured board, roll half the dough into a 9 x 13 inch (23 x 33 cm) rectangle. Cut into 1½ inch (4 cm) squares. Spoon 1 tbsp (15 mL) of filling onto half of squares and cover with remaining squares. Press edges together with a fork to seal. Repeat with remaining dough.

- Arrange cookies on ungreased cookie sheet and bake 10 minutes. Transfer to wire racks and let cool.

GINGER ROUNDS
(4 dozen)

½ cup	vegetable shortening	125 mL
¾ cup	granulated sugar	175 mL
1	egg	1
2 tbsp	milk	30 mL
2 cups	all-purpose flour	500 mL
1½ tsp	ground ginger	7 mL
½ cup	ginger marmalade	125 mL

- In a large bowl, cream shortening with sugar until light and fluffy. Add egg and milk; blend thoroughly. Sift flour with ginger. Add to creamed mixture and mix well.

- Knead dough several times until smooth. Chill 1 hour in refrigerator.

- Preheat oven to 350°F (180°C); lightly grease cookie sheets.

- Roll dough to about ⅛ inch (3 mm) thickness. Cut into rounds, about 1½ inch (3.5 cm) in diameter, or into other shapes with different cookie cutters.

- Arrange on cookie sheet and bake 10 to 12 minutes until golden. When done, transfer to wire racks and let cool.

- Top half of cookies with ginger marmalade, then cover with remaining cookies to make sandwiches.

PEEK-A-BOOS
(2 dozen)

¾ cup	unsalted butter	175 mL
1 cup	granulated sugar	250 mL
1	egg	1
½ tsp	vanilla extract	2 mL
1 cup	all-purpose flour	250 mL
¾ cup	whole wheat flour	175 mL
1	egg white	1
¾ cup	mixed orange and lemon peel, finely chopped	175 mL

- In a large bowl, cream butter with sugar. Add egg and vanilla, and beat until well-blended. Gradually fold in flours, working by hand until fully blended. Chill dough 1 hour in refrigerator.

- Preheat oven to 350°F (180°C); Grease and flour a cookie sheet.

- On floured board, roll dough out about ¼ inch (5 mm) thick. Cut into 2 inch (5 cm) squares and transfer half of them to cookie sheet. Brush with lightly beaten egg white and place a small spoonful of mixed peel in the center of each square.

- Cut a ½ inch (1 cm) opening in remaining squares. Place on top of squares with filling, pressing edges together to seal.

- Bake 12 to 15 minutes, or until golden. Transfer cookies to wire racks and let cool.

VARIATION: *Fill with puréed dates or figs instead of mixed peel.*

THIMBLE COOKIES
(3½ dozen)

½ cup	unsalted butter	125 mL
4 oz	cream cheese	125 g
¾ cup	granulated sugar	175 mL
1	egg	1
2 cups	all-purpose flour	500 mL
½ tsp	baking powder	2 mL
¾ cup	finely chopped almonds	175 mL
	raspberry jam	
	apricot jam	

- Preheat oven to 350°F (180°C); lightly grease cookie sheets.

- In a large bowl, cream butter and cream cheese with sugar. Add egg and blend well. Sift flour with baking powder. Stir in almonds and add to creamed mixture.

- Knead dough gently until smooth.

- Pull off pieces of dough to make 1 inch (2.5 cm) balls. Place on cookie sheet and make an indentation in center of each ball with a floured sewing thimble.

- Bake 10 minutes and remove from oven. Press thimble into the center of each cookie again and return to oven. Bake 8 to 10 minutes longer until golden. When done, transfer cookies to wire racks and let cool.

- Fill centers with a small amount of jam. Store overnight in an airtight container before serving.

DATE SURPRISES

(2½ dozen)

¾ cup	pitted dates (about 15)	175 mL
2 tbsp	blanched slivered almonds	30 mL
¾ cup	unsalted butter	175 mL
1 cup	granulated sugar	250 mL
1	egg	1
⅛ tsp	almond extract	0.5 mL
1 cup	all-purpose flour	250 mL
1 cup	whole wheat flour	250 mL
	coarse sugar	

- Preheat oven to 375°F (190°C). Grease and flour a cookie sheet.
- Stuff each date with 2 slivers of almond. Cut crosswise in half and set aside.
- In a large bowl, cream butter with sugar. Add egg and almond extract, and beat until well-blended. Gradually fold in flours, working with hands until fully blended. On well-floured board, knead dough until smooth.
- Pull off pieces of dough the size of walnuts. Roll into balls, then flatten. Press half a date into the center of each, then form dough around date and into a ball. Roll in coarse sugar.
- Bake for 10 to 12 minutes, until firm and golden. Transfer to wire racks and let cool.

Stuff each date with 2 slivers of almond. Cut crosswise in half.

Pull off pieces of dough the size of walnuts. Roll into balls, then flatten.

Press half a date into the center of each, then form dough around date and into a ball.

JELLY SANDWICH COOKIES
(3 dozen)

¾ cup	unsalted butter or margarine	175 mL
1 cup	granulated sugar	250 mL
1 tsp	vanilla extract	5 mL
1	egg	1
2½ cups	all-purpose flour	625 mL
2 tsp	baking powder	10 mL
½ cup	milk	125 mL
	pinch of salt	
	choice of fruit jelly	
	confectioners' sugar	

- In a large bowl, cream together butter and sugar. Add vanilla and egg; mix well.

- Sift together flour, baking powder and salt. Gradually stir dry ingredients into butter mixture, alternating with milk, and ending with dry ingredients. Chill dough 1 hour in refrigerator.

- Preheat oven to 375°F (190°C). Grease a cookie sheet.

- Roll dough and cut cookies with a round cookie cutter. Using a smaller cookie cutter, cut a hole into half the cookies. Arrange on cookie sheet and bake about 10 minutes.

- Top whole cookies with fruit jelly and cover each one with a cookie that has a hole in it. Sprinkle with confectioners' sugar, if desired.

HOLIDAY COOKIES

As a holiday approaches, many people are already excited at the thought of making all kinds of special treats. Often, just the choice of cookies, their shapes and decorations, is a party in itself.

Passed on from generation to generation, many of these recipes are part of family traditions and happy times. Now you can relive these traditions or even create new ones!

ROSETTES

(1½ dozen)

1 cup	all-purpose flour	250 mL
2 tbsp	granulated sugar	30 mL
¼ tsp	salt	1 mL
2	eggs	2
½ cup	whipping cream	125 mL
½ cup	milk	125 mL
1 tsp	vanilla extract	5 mL
	peanut oil for deep-frying	
	confectioners' sugar	

- In a medium bowl, combine flour, granulated sugar and salt; mix well. Add eggs, cream, milk and vanilla, blending until smooth.

- In a large heavy saucepan or deep-fryer, heat oil to 375°F (190°C). Preheat rosette iron in oil according to manufacturer's directions.

- Dip hot iron into batter, being sure not to coat top side of forms with batter. Then dip iron into hot oil until rosette is golden, about 30 to 45 seconds. Gently remove rosette from iron with a fork and drain on paper towels. Repeat with remaining batter.

- When rosettes are cool, sprinkle with confectioners' sugar.

CINNAMON CHRISTMAS STARS

(4 dozen)

¼ cup	brown sugar	50 mL
½ cup	granulated sugar	125 mL
½ cup	unsalted butter, softened	125 mL
¼ cup	vegetable shortening	50 mL
1 tsp	vanilla extract	5 mL
2	eggs	2
2¾ cups	all-purpose flour	675 mL
1 tsp	baking powder	5 mL
¼ tsp	salt	1 mL
¼ cup	granulated sugar	50 mL
½ tsp	cinnamon	2 mL

- In a large bowl, mix together brown sugar, ½ cup (125 mL) granulated sugar, butter, shortening, vanilla and eggs. Stir in flour, baking powder and salt. Cover and chill at least 1 hour in refrigerator.

- Preheat oven to 400°F (200°C).

- Roll dough ⅛ inch (3 mm) thick. Shape cookies with a 2½ inch (6 cm) star-shaped cookie cutter. Cut a ¼ inch (5 mm) slit between 2 points on each star, cutting just past the center, and place on ungreased cookie sheet.

- Mix together ¼ cup (50 mL) granulated sugar and cinnamon; sprinkle over cookies. Bake 6 to 8 minutes until golden. Let cool about 1 minute, then transfer to wire racks and let cool completely. Fit cookies together, two by two at the slits.

VALENTINE SANDWICHES

(2 dozen)

⅓ cup	vegetable shortening	75 mL
¾ cup	granulated sugar	175 mL
1	egg	1
1 tbsp	lemon juice	15 mL
1¼ cups	all-purpose flour	300 mL
½ cup	raspberry or strawberry jam	125 mL
	confectioners' sugar	

ICING

1 tbsp	vegetable shortening	15 mL
1 cup	confectioners' sugar	250 mL
2-3 tsp	milk	10-15 mL

- In a large bowl, cream shortening with sugar. Add egg and lemon juice; beat well. Gradually add flour, mixing well after each addition. Chill dough for about 2 hours until firm.

- Preheat oven to 375°F (190°C). Grease cookie sheets.

- Working with half the dough at a time, roll out on floured board as thinly as possible. Cut into heart shapes using two different-sized cookie cutters, place on cookie sheet and bake 8 to 10 minutes, until beginning to harden. Do not let cookies brown. Transfer to wire racks and let cool.

- To prepare icing, cream shortening with sugar. Add just enough milk to make icing spreadable.

- When hearts are completely cool, spread jam and icing on bigger cookies, then cover with smaller cookies. Sprinkle with confectioners' sugar if desired.

HAZELNUT BISCOTTI
(3 dozen)

3	eggs	3
½ cup	hazelnut or vegetable oil	125 mL
1 cup	granulated sugar	250 mL
½ cup	finely chopped hazelnuts	125 mL
2¼ cups	all-purpose flour	550 mL
2 tsp	baking powder	10 mL

- Preheat oven to 350°F (180°C). Grease and flour a cookie sheet.

- In a large bowl, beat eggs with oil; add sugar and continue beating about 5 minutes, until mixture is thick and pale. Fold in chopped hazelnuts.

- Sift flour with baking powder. Add to egg mixture and mix using wooden spoon or hands.

- Shape dough into 2 logs about 3 x 10 inches (7.5 x 25 cm). Arrange on cookie sheet. Using a wet spatula, flatten top and smooth sides of logs.

- Bake 25 to 30 minutes until golden. Remove from oven and lower oven temperature to 300°F (150°C). Let logs cool on cookie sheet about 10 minutes. Cut into ½ inch (1 cm) slices using serrated knife.

- Arrange slices flat on cookie sheet and bake 15 minutes longer, until surface is dry and crisp. Transfer cookies to wire racks and let cool. Store in airtight container.

Using a wet spatula, flatten top and smooth sides of logs.

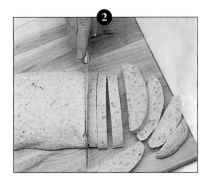

Once baked, cut into ½ inch (1 cm) slices using serrated knife.

Arrange slices flat on cookie sheet and bake 15 minutes longer.

CHRISTMAS COOKIES

(2½ dozen)

¾ cup	unsalted butter	175 mL
½ cup	granulated sugar	125 mL
2 tbsp	marzipan	30 mL
1	egg	1
1 cup	crushed crispy rice cereal	250 mL
1½ cups	all-purpose flour	375 mL
	red and green food coloring	
	colored sugar	

- Preheat oven to 350°F (180°C). Lightly grease cookie sheets.

- In a large bowl, cream butter with sugar. Soften marzipan with a fork and blend into creamed mixture. Add egg, rice cereal, then flour, mixing well after each addition.

- Divide dough into 3 portions, adding red food coloring to one and green to another. Turn each portion onto well-floured board, kneading a few times until dough becomes elastic.

- Roll dough, one portion at a time, on floured board, about ¼ inch (5 mm) thick. Cut into Christmas shapes with different cookie cutters. Decorate with colored sugar and arrange on cookie sheet. Bake 8 to 10 minutes until firm. Do not let cookies brown.

- When done, transfer to wire racks and let cool.

165

ℬIRSCH FINGERS

(2 dozen)

⅔ cup	confectioners' sugar	150 mL
2	egg whites	2
1 tsp	kirsch liqueur	5 mL
½ tsp	lemon juice	2 mL
7 oz	puff pastry	200 g

- Preheat oven to 400°F (200°C).

- Prepare the icing: with a spatula, combine confectioners' sugar, egg whites, kirsch and lemon juice.

- Roll puff pastry into a 6 x 12 inch (15 x 30 cm) rectangle. Cover pastry with icing and cut in half to make two 3 x 12 inch (7.5 x 30 cm) strips. Slice into ¾ inch (2 cm) wide fingers.

- Place fingers on an ungreased cookie sheet and bake 8 to 10 minutes. Let cool before serving.

COCONUT RUM GEMS

(3 dozen)

1 cup	all-purpose flour	250 mL
1 cup	crushed corn flakes	250 mL
¾ cup	granulated sugar	175 mL
½ cup	chopped nuts	125 mL
½ cup	flaked coconut	125 mL
½ cup	chopped orange and lemon peel	125 mL
2	eggs	2
1 tbsp	rum	15 mL
	shredded coconut	

- Preheat oven to 350°F (180°C); lightly grease cookie sheets.

- In a large bowl, mix together flour, corn flakes, sugar, nuts, coconut and peel.

- In another bowl, beat eggs with rum; blend into dry ingredients.

- Drop small spoonfuls of batter into shredded coconut. Shape into 1 inch (2.5 cm) balls and place on cookie sheet. Bake 10 to 12 minutes, or until firm.

- When done, transfer to wire racks and let cool.

HALLOWEEN STAINED GLASS COOKIES

(6 dozen)

¾ cup	granulated sugar	175 mL
½ cup	unsalted butter, softened	125 mL
¼ cup	vegetable shortening	50 mL
1 tsp	vanilla extract	5 mL
2	eggs	2
2¾ cups	all-purpose flour	675 mL
1 tsp	baking powder	5 mL
¼ tsp	salt	1 mL
	hard candies of assorted colors	

• In a medium bowl, combine sugar, butter, shortening, vanilla and eggs. Stir in flour, baking powder and salt. Cover and chill at least 1 hour in refrigerator.

• Preheat oven to 375°F (190°C). Line cookie sheet with aluminum foil.

• On a floured board, roll dough out ⅛ inch (3 mm) thick. Cut into Halloween shapes with different cookie cutters and arrange on cookie sheet. Decorate (eyes, mouth, etc.) with hard candies, whole or in pieces.*

• Bake 7 to 9 minutes, until edges of cookies are golden and candies melt. Let cookies cool completely on cookie sheet.

*To crush candies, place between two paper towels and tap lightly. Because they melt easily, it is best to keep pieces as large as possible.

168

*C*HOCOLATE MACAROONS
(2 dozen)

2	egg whites	2
1 cup	granulated sugar	250 mL
½ tsp	almond extract	2 mL
½ cup	finely ground almonds	125 mL
½ cup	unsweetened shredded coconut	125 mL
¼ cup	cocoa powder	50 mL

ও

- Preheat oven to 325°F (160°C); grease and flour cookie sheets.

- In a large bowl, beat egg whites until frothy. Gradually add sugar and continue beating until stiff peaks form. Stir in almond extract.

- In another bowl, combine ground almonds, coconut and cocoa. Gently fold into egg whites.

- Drop small spoonfuls of batter onto cookie sheet, 1 inch (2.5 cm) apart. Bake 12 to 15 minutes until tops of macaroons are firm. Let cool on cookie sheet a few minutes, then gently remove to wire rack and let cool completely. Store in an airtight container.

EASTER CELEBRATION COOKIES
(3 dozen)

1 cup	unsalted butter, softened	250 mL
1 cup	brown sugar	250 mL
1	egg	1
1 tsp	vanilla extract	5 mL
2½ cups	all-purpose flour	625 mL
1 tsp	baking powder	5 mL
2	squares semi-sweet baking chocolate, melted	2
	assorted cake decorations (sprinkles, rainbow bits, miniature chips, etc.)	
	colored coarse sugar	
	icing	

- In a large bowl, cream butter with brown sugar until light and fluffy. Stir in egg and vanilla. Combine flour and baking powder; add to creamed mixture.

- Divide dough in half and add melted chocolate to 1 portion. Cover and chill both portions separately 1 hour in refrigerator.

- Preheat oven to 350°F (180°C). Grease a cookie sheet.

- On a lightly floured board, roll each portion of dough about ¼ inch (5 mm) thick. Cut cookies into Easter shapes (rabbits, eggs, flowers, etc.). Arrange on cookie sheet, about 1 inch (2.5 cm) apart. If desired, sprinkle some of cookies with coarse sugar before or after baking them.

- Bake 7 to 8 minutes, until edges are lightly browned. Let cool before decorating.

MINI RASPBERRY PINWHEELS

(6 dozen)

½ cup	unsalted butter	125 mL
4 oz	cream cheese	125 g
1 cup	granulated sugar	250 mL
1	egg	1
1 tsp	lemon juice	5 mL
1 tbsp	chopped lemon zest	15 mL
2¼ cups	all-purpose flour	550 mL
½ tsp	baking soda	2 mL
1 cup	raspberry jam	250 mL

- In a large bowl, cream butter and cream cheese with sugar. Add egg, juice and lemon zest; continue beating until light and fluffy.

- Sift flour and baking soda together. Gradually add to creamed mixture, blending after each addition. Chill for 1 hour.

- Preheat oven to 350°F (180°C); lightly grease cookie sheets.

- Divide dough in three. Working on floured board, roll 1 portion into a rectangle, about 9 x 10 inches (23 x 25 cm) and ⅛ inch (3 mm) thick. Trim edges. Brush with ⅓ of raspberry jam and roll up. Repeat with remaining portions of dough and jam.

- Cut rolls into slices and place on cookie sheet. Bake for 10 to 12 minutes, or until firm. When done, transfer to wire racks and let cool.

On a floured board, roll 1 portion into a rectangle, about 9 x 10 inches (23 x 25 cm) and ⅛ inch (3 mm) thick. Trim edges.

Brush with ⅓ of raspberry jam and roll up.

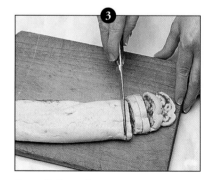

Cut rolls into slices.

CHOCOLATE COCONUT CHERRY DROPS
(2 dozen)

⅓ cup	vegetable shortening	75 mL
½ cup	granulated sugar	125 mL
1	egg	1
½ tsp	almond extract	2 mL
¾ cup	all-purpose flour	175 mL
½ tsp	baking powder	2 mL
¾ cup	semi-sweet chocolate chips	175 mL
½ cup	shredded coconut	125 mL
½ cup	chopped maraschino cherries	125 mL

- Preheat oven to 325°F (160°C). Grease a cookie sheet.

- In a large bowl, cream shortening with sugar. Beat in egg, almond extract, flour and baking powder. Add remaining ingredients and mix well.

- Drop spoonfuls of dough onto cookie sheet and bake 15 to 17 minutes. Transfer to wire racks and let cool.

 OCHA RUM BALLS

(2½ dozen)

2 cups	ground ginger snaps	500 mL
1 cup	confectioners' sugar	250 mL
½ cup	shredded coconut	125 mL
½ cup	finely chopped walnuts	125 mL
2 tbsp	cocoa powder	30 mL
1 tsp	instant coffee crystals	5 mL
1 tbsp	boiling water	15 mL
2 tbsp	corn syrup	30 mL
4 tbsp	coconut-rum liqueur	60 mL
	confectioners' sugar	
	cocoa powder	

- Combine ginger crumbs, confectioners' sugar, coconut, walnuts and cocoa.

- In a small saucepan, dissolve instant coffee in boiling water. Add syrup and heat gently until blended. Mix with dry ingredients using tips of fingers.

- Add only enough liqueur to hold ingredients together when squeezed.

- Shape dough into 1 inch (2.5 cm) balls and roll either in confectioners' sugar or cocoa powder.

- Store in an airtight container until flavors blend (at least 1 day; 1 week if possible). If desired, roll again in confectioners' sugar or cocoa just before serving.

CHOCOLATE AND RASPBERRY ROUNDABOUTS

(4 dozen)

1	square unsweetened baking chocolate	1
½ cup	unsalted butter	125 mL
½ cup	vegetable shortening	125 mL
1 cup	granulated sugar	250 mL
1	egg	1
1 tsp	raspberry or vanilla extract	5 mL
5 drops	red food coloring	5 drops
2 cups	all-purpose flour	500 mL
1	egg white	1

- Melt chocolate over hot water. Set aside to cool.

- In a large bowl, cream butter and shortening with sugar until light and fluffy. Add egg, raspberry extract and food coloring; blend well. Gradually add flour, working the last bit in by hand, if necessary.

- Knead dough on floured board until smooth. Divide into 2 portions. Add melted chocolate to 1 portion. Wrap both portions separately in waxed paper and chill about 4 hours in refrigerator.

- Roll red portion into a log, about 12 inches (30 cm) long. Roll chocolate portion into a rectangle, about 6 x 12 inches (15 x 30 cm).

- Brush rectangle with slightly beaten egg white. Place log on rectangle. Wrap log with chocolate dough, and brush edges with egg white before sealing. Wrap in waxed paper and chill about 2 hours.

- Preheat oven to 375°F (190°C). Cut dough into ¼ inch (5 mm) thick slices. Place on ungreased cookie sheet, about 1 inch (2.5 cm) apart.

- Bake 8 to 10 minutes, or until firm. Transfer to wire racks and let cool.

MINI PALMIERS

(3 dozen)

7 oz	puff pastry	200 g
⅓ cup	confectioners' sugar	75 mL

- Preheat oven to 400°F (200°C).

- On a work surface sprinkled with confectioners' sugar, roll pastry into a 8 x 16 inch (20 x 40 cm) rectangle. Fold the long sides of the rectangle in towards the center, sprinkle with confectioners' sugar and fold this strip in half to make 4 layers altogether.

- Chill pastry in freezer 5 minutes, then cut into ¼ inch (5 mm) thick slices. Place flat on an ungreased cookie sheet, about 2 inches (5 cm) apart.

- Bake in oven, 6 minutes on one side and 3 minutes on the other. Let cool before serving.

On a work surface sprinkled with confectioners' sugar, roll pastry into a 8 x 16 inch (20 x 40 cm) rectangle.

Fold the long sides of the rectangle in towards the center.

Fold this strip in half to make 4 layers.

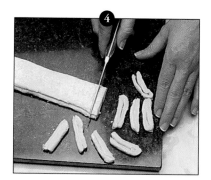

Cut dough into ¼ inch (5 mm) thick slices.

178

BLACK AND WHITE CHECKERBOARDS

(3½ dozen)

¼ cup	vegetable shortening	50 mL
½ cup	unsalted butter, softened	125 mL
1 cup	granulated sugar	250 mL
1 tsp	vanilla extract	5 mL
¼ tsp	salt	1 mL
1	egg	1
2 cups	all-purpose flour	500 mL
2	squares unsweetened baking chocolate, melted and cooled	2
2	squares white baking chocolate, melted and cooled	2
1	egg white	1
2 tsp	water	10 mL

- In a large bowl, beat shortening, butter, sugar, vanilla and salt until light and fluffy. Beat in egg. Stir in flour, ½ cup (125 mL) at a time, mixing well after each addition.

- Divide dough in half. Blend melted unsweetened chocolate into 1 portion, and white chocolate into the other. Wrap each portion in plastic and chill 1 hour in refrigerator.

- Beat egg white with water, and set aside. On a floured board, roll white chocolate dough into a rectangle, ½ inch (1 cm) thick. Cut into 9 strips, about ½ inch (1 cm) wide and 5½ inches (13.5 cm) long. Repeat rolling and cutting with dark chocolate dough.

- To make the checkerboards, place three strips, alternating dark and light, side by side and touching, on a large piece of plastic wrap. Brush the top lightly with egg white. Place 3 more strips on top, a light strip over a dark strip, a dark strip over a light strip. Brush with egg white. Create a third layer, always alternating colors.

- Press sides and top to make one smooth log. Fold excess plastic wrap over log to seal. Repeat with remaining 9 strips of dough to make a second log. Chill overnight in refrigerator.

- Preheat oven to 325°F (160°C). Lightly grease 2 cookie sheets.

- Remove one log from refrigerator at a time and cut into ¼ inch (5 mm) slices. Arrange on cookie sheet, about 1 inch (2.5 cm) apart. Repeat with remaining log.

- Bake 12 minutes, or until bottoms of cookies are golden brown. Transfer to wire racks and let cool. Checkerboards will keep 1 week in an airtight container at room temperature or they can be frozen.

Meringue Cookies

(3 dozen)

3	egg whites	3
1¼ cups	superfine sugar	300 mL
1 tsp	vanilla extract	5 mL
	pinch of salt	

- Preheat oven to 250°F (120°C). Grease and flour a cookie sheet.

- Place egg whites in copper or stainless steel bowl. Add salt and beat until stiff. Beating constantly, gradually add sugar and vanilla.

- Drop tablespoonfuls (15 mL) of batter onto prepared cookie sheet and bake 60 minutes.

INTERNATIONAL COOKIES

As part of the "global village," we discover new cooking customs and specialties from around the world every day.

With their novel shapes, textures and flavors, the cookies in this chapter are sure to awaken a desire for travel and discovery. For globe-trotters, they may evoke fond memories, while for others, they are sure to conjure up images of the old country.

ALMOND BISCOTTI

(3 dozen)

3	eggs	3
½ cup	vegetable oil	125 mL
1 cup	granulated sugar	250 mL
2 tsp	almond extract	10 mL
½ cup	finely chopped almonds	125 mL
2½ cups	all-purpose flour	625 mL
2 tsp	baking powder	10 mL

- Preheat oven to 350°F (180°C); grease and flour cookie sheet.

- In a large bowl, beat eggs with oil; add sugar and almond extract. Continue beating about 5 minutes until mixture is thick and pale. Fold in chopped almonds.

- Sift flour with baking powder. Stir into egg mixture using wooden spoon then hands, if necessary.

- Shape dough into 2 logs about 3 x 10 inches (7.5 x 25 cm) each, and arrange on cookie sheet. Using a wet spatula, flatten top and smooth sides of logs.

- Bake 25 to 30 minutes until golden. Remove from oven and lower oven temperature to 300°F (150°C).

- Let logs cool on cookie sheet about 10 minutes. Cut into ½ inch (1 cm) slices using serrated knife. Lay slices flat on cookie sheet and bake 20 minutes longer, until surface is golden and crisp.

- When done, transfer cookies to wire racks and let cool. Store in airtight container.

VARIATION: *For Lemon Biscotti, reduce almond extract to 1 tsp (5 mL) and add 1 tbsp (15 mL) grated lemon rind to egg mixture.*

SCOTTISH OAT BISCUITS
(1½ dozen)

1	large egg	1
½ cup	superfine sugar	125 mL
1 tbsp	melted butter	15 mL
½ tsp	vanilla extract	2 mL
1 cup	oatmeal flakes	250 mL
	pinch of salt	

- Preheat oven to 325°F (160°C). Butter and lightly flour cookie sheets.

- Beat egg in large bowl until fluffy. Gradually add sugar, beating constantly.

- Stir in remaining ingredients.

- Drop small spoonfuls of batter onto cookie sheets. Bake 15 minutes or according to size.

- When done, transfer cookies to wire racks and let cool.

Scottish Shortbread
(2 dozen)

1 cup	butter, softened	250 mL
1 cup	superfine sugar	250 mL
2½ cups	all-purpose flour	625 mL

- Preheat oven to 275°F (140°C).

- Cream butter in large bowl. Add sugar and mix well with wooden spoon.

- Gradually add flour, kneading dough on work surface. When dough no longer sticks to surface, roll out ¼ inch (5 mm) thick.

- Cut out shapes with cookie cutter. Arrange cookies on ungreased cookie sheets. Bake 45 to 50 minutes, until cookies are lightly browned.

- When done, transfer cookies to wire racks and let cool.

SPRINGERLE
(4 dozen)

3	eggs	3
1¾ cups	granulated sugar	425 mL
1 tbsp	orange juice concentrate	15 mL
1 tsp	grated orange rind	5 mL
2½ cups	all-purpose flour	625 mL
½ tsp	baking powder	2 mL
1 tbsp	anise seeds	15 mL

- In a large bowl, beat eggs with sugar 6 to 8 minutes, until thick and creamy. Add orange juice concentrate and rind; mix well.

- Sift flour with baking powder. Gradually add to egg mixture, kneading in the last of the flour by hand.

- Lightly grease 2 large cookie sheets; sprinkle with anise seeds.

- Flour a carved springerle rolling pin; roll half of dough on floured board about ¼ inch (5 mm) thick, and slightly wider than rolling pin, pressing patterns into dough.

- Cut cookies along lines between patterns and transfer to cookie sheets. Repeat with remaining dough and let stand overnight in cool, dry place.

- Preheat oven to 300°F (150°C).

- Bake cookies 15 to 20 minutes until tops are crisp and bottoms are golden. When done, transfer to wire racks and let cool. Store in airtight container for 1 week to soften.

Flour a springerle rolling pin and roll dough to make patterns.

Cut cookies along lines separating patterns.

Transfer to greased cookie sheets sprinkled with anise seeds.

FORTUNE COOKIES

(2 dozen)

1 cup	all-purpose flour	250 mL
2 tbsp	corn starch	30 mL
½ cup	granulated sugar	125 mL
½ cup	vegetable oil	125 mL
2 tsp	water	10 mL
½ tsp	almond extract	2 mL
4	egg whites	4
	red and yellow food coloring	

- Write predictions or proverbs on pieces of paper, about ½ x 3 inches (1 x 7.5 cm).

- Preheat oven to 375°F (190°C); thoroughly grease 2 small cookie sheets.

- Combine flour, corn starch and sugar in a large bowl. Stir in oil, water and almond extract. Add egg whites, 1 drop of red coloring and 2 drops of yellow coloring, blending thoroughly after each addition.

- Drop one small spoonful of batter onto cookie sheet. Spread batter into a circle, about 3 inches (7.5 cm) in diameter. Only bake one cookie at a time. Bake 4 minutes just until firm on top. Do not brown.

- Place message on cookie. Lift cookie with spatula and quickly but gently fold in half, then fold in the other direction. Hold in place with spatula a few seconds until cool.

- Continue with remaining batter, baking one cookie at a time, using both cookie sheets. Batter should not be put on warm cookie sheet. Store fortune cookies in an airtight container.

ALMOND COOKIES

(2½ dozen)

1¾ cups	all-purpose flour	425 mL
1 cup	granulated sugar	250 mL
1 tsp	baking powder	5 mL
½ cup	vegetable shortening	125 mL
2	eggs (1 whole, 1 separated)	2
1½ tsp	almond extract	7 mL
1 tsp	water	5 mL
⅓ cup	whole blanched almonds	75 mL

- Preheat oven to 350°F (180°C).

- In a bowl, sift flour with sugar and baking powder. Cut in shortening until mixture resembles coarse bread crumbs. With wooden spoon, stir in whole egg, egg white and almond extract. Mixture should be very crumbly.

- Turn out onto floured board, and knead until ingredients are thoroughly blended, and dough is smooth and shiny. Pull off pieces of dough and roll into 1¼ inch (3 cm) balls. Arrange 1 inch (2.5 cm) apart on ungreased cookie sheet and flatten slightly.

- Mix egg yolk with water and brush each cookie well. Press whole almond firmly into center of each cookie.

- Bake 15 minutes or until golden. When done, transfer to wire racks and let cool.

Sesame Cookies

(4 dozen)

1 cup	sesame seeds	250 mL
2	eggs	2
½ cup	granulated sugar	125 mL
½ cup	vegetable oil	125 mL
2 tsp	lemon juice	10 mL
2⅛ cups	all-purpose flour	525 mL
	vegetable oil	

- Preheat oven to 325°F (160°C).

- Toast sesame seeds in ungreased frying pan over low heat, stirring frequently until golden.

- In a large bowl, beat eggs with sugar and oil until thick. Add lemon juice and flour to mixture, working the flour in by hand, if necessary.

- Roll dough into a large ball. Pinch off small pieces of dough the size of walnuts. Oil hands, and roll each piece into a ball, then roll each ball in toasted sesame seeds.

- Arrange balls on ungreased cookie sheet and bake 15 to 20 minutes until golden. When done, transfer to wire racks and let cool.

KOURABIEDES
(4 dozen)

1 cup	unsalted butter	250 mL
½ cup	granulated sugar	125 mL
1	egg	1
½ tsp	vanilla extract	2 mL
¼ tsp	almond extract	1 mL
½ tsp	allspice	2 mL
½ tsp	cinnamon	2 mL
1 tsp	baking powder	5 mL
2 cups	all-purpose flour	500 mL
¾ cup	finely ground almonds	175 mL
	confectioners' sugar	

- Cream butter with sugar in a large bowl. Add egg, vanilla and almond extracts, allspice and cinnamon; blend well.

- Mix together baking powder and flour and gradually work into butter mixture. When too stiff for mixer, use wooden spoon or fingers. Knead well until all flour is mixed in. Chill for 1 hour in refrigerator.

- Preheat oven to 350°F (180°C).

- Pull off small pieces of dough the size of walnuts. Roll into a ball, then roll into cylinders.

- Roll each piece in ground almonds and curve into a crescent shape. Bake on ungreased cookie sheet 25 minutes or until firm. Transfer to wire racks and let cool. Sprinkle with confectioners' sugar before serving.

PFEFFERNÜSSE

(2½ dozen)

¼ cup	vegetable shortening	50 mL
½ cup	granulated sugar	125 mL
2	eggs	2
1 tsp	grated orange zest	5 mL
½ cup	finely chopped almonds	125 mL
½ cup	chopped candied fruit	125 mL
2 cups	all-purpose flour	500 mL
½ tsp	baking powder	2 mL
2 tsp	cinnamon	10 mL
½ tsp	ground cardamom	2 mL
½ tsp	allspice	2 mL
½ tsp	ground nutmeg	2 mL
	pinch of pepper	
	confectioners' sugar	

- Cream shortening with sugar in a large bowl. Add eggs; beat until light and fluffy. Add orange zest, almonds and candied fruit.

- Sift flour with baking powder, cinnamon, cardamom, allspice, nutmeg and pepper. Gradually work into egg mixture, first with mixer or wooden spoon, then with hands. Chill 1 hour in refrigerator.

- Preheat oven to 350°F (180°C). Grease a cookie sheet.

- Shape dough into 1 inch (2.5 cm) balls and arrange on cookie sheet. Bake 15 to 20 minutes until firm. While still warm, roll in sifted confectioners' sugar, if desired. Let cool and store in airtight container.

MAPLE LEAF COOKIES
(4 dozen)

½ cup	unsalted butter	125 mL
¾ cup	maple syrup	175 mL
1	egg	1
2¼ cups	all-purpose flour	550 mL

ICING

1 tbsp	unsalted butter	15 mL
1 cup	sifted confectioners' sugar	250 mL
½ tsp	maple extract	2 mL
3-4 tbsp	heavy cream	45-60 mL

- Cream butter until fluffy. Gradually blend in maple syrup and egg. Fold in flour and stir gently. Chill for 1 hour in refrigerator.

- Preheat oven to 350°F (180°C); lightly grease cookie sheets.

- Roll dough out on well-floured board about ¼ inch (5 mm) thick. Cut out maple leaf shapes with a cookie cutter and bake 8 to 10 minutes until golden. When done, transfer cookies to wire racks and let cool.

- To prepare icing, cream butter with sugar. Add maple extract, then cream, 1 teaspoon (5 mL) at a time, to obtain desired consistency.

- Spread icing onto half of cookies, then cover with remaining cookies to make sandwiches.

Roll dough out on well-floured board, about ¼ inch (5 mm) thick.

Cut out maple leaf shapes with a cookie cutter and arrange on cookie sheet.

To prepare icing, cream butter with sugar. Add maple extract, then cream to obtain desired consistency.

Spread icing onto half of cookies, then cover with remaining cookies to make sandwiches.

LADYFINGERS

(2½ dozen)

3	eggs, separated	3
5 tbsp	granulated sugar	75 mL
½ tsp	orange juice concentrate	2 mL
½ cup	all-purpose flour	125 mL
	confectioners' sugar	

- Preheat oven to 350°F (180°C); grease and flour cookie sheets.

- Beat egg whites just until foamy. Add 2 tablespoons (30 mL) sugar, one at a time. Continue to beat until soft, shiny peaks form.

- In another bowl, beat egg yolks with remaining 3 tbsp (45 mL) sugar until thick and lemon-colored, about 5 minutes. Add orange juice concentrate.

- Gently fold half the flour into the yolks. Fold some yolk mixture into whites, then fold all egg white mixture into yolks. Fold in remaining flour.

- Spoon mixture into pastry bag with ¾ inch (2 cm) opening. Pipe fingers 4 inches (10 cm) long onto cookie sheet, 1 inch (2.5 cm) apart. Sift confectioners' sugar over fingers and bake 10 to 12 minutes until firm and slightly golden.

- Transfer to wire racks and let cool. Store in airtight containers.

SACHER COOKIES
(3 dozen)

2	squares unsweetened baking chocolate	2
⅓ cup	vegetable shortening	75 mL
¾ cup	granulated sugar	175 mL
1	egg	1
1 tbsp	coffee	15 mL
1½ cups	all-purpose flour	375 mL
1 cup	apricot jam	250 mL
1½ cups	whipping cream	375 mL
¼ tsp	vanilla extract	1 mL
	cocoa powder	

- Preheat oven to 350°F (180°C). Lightly grease cookie sheets.

- Melt chocolate over hot water. Set aside to cool.

- In a large bowl, cream shortening with sugar; blend in egg, coffee, then melted chocolate. Gradually mix in flour, kneading until smooth.

- Turn dough out on well-floured board and roll out ¼ inch (5 mm) thick.

- Cut out circles, about 2 inches (5 cm) in diameter. Bake 8 to 10 minutes until firm. Transfer cookies to wire racks and let cool.

- When ready to serve, spread apricot jam on each cookie. Whip cream with vanilla until doubled in volume; spoon a dollop of whipped cream on top of each cookie and sprinkle with cocoa.

LEBKUCHEN
(3 dozen)

½ cup	molasses	125 mL
½ cup	honey	125 mL
1 cup	brown sugar	250 mL
2 tbsp	vegetable shortening	30 mL
2 tbsp	water	30 mL
½ cup	finely chopped walnuts	125 mL
¼ cup	chopped candied peel	50 mL
3 cups	all-purpose flour	750 mL
½ tsp	baking soda	2 mL
1 tsp	cinnamon	5 mL
½ tsp	ground clove	2 mL
¼ tsp	ground ginger	1 mL
¼ tsp	ground nutmeg	1 mL

GLAZE

½ cup	sifted confectioners' sugar	125 mL
2 tsp	warm water	10 mL
1 tsp	lemon juice	5 mL

- Preheat oven to 325°F (160°C); grease cookie sheets.

- In a large saucepan, combine molasses, honey, brown sugar, shortening and water. Place over low heat and bring to a boil, stirring constantly. Remove from heat and stir in nuts and peel. Let cool.

- Sift flour with baking soda, cinnamon, clove, ginger and nutmeg. Gradually add to molasses mixture and stir well.

- Turn dough out onto a floured board, and knead, adding extra flour if necessary to prevent sticking.

- Roll dough ¼ inch (5 mm) thick. Cut into 1 x 3 inch (2.5 x 7.5 cm) rectangles and arrange on cookie sheets.

- Bake 18 to 20 minutes until firm. When done, transfer cookies to wire racks and let cool.

- To prepare glaze, stir water and lemon juice into confectioners' sugar. Brush glaze onto warm cookies and let harden.

- Store in airtight container with a piece of orange rind for about 1 week until cookies soften.

MADELEINES

(1½ dozen)

⅔ cup	**unsalted butter**	150 mL
3	**eggs**	3
1 cup	**sifted confectioners' sugar**	250 mL
2 tsp	**grated lemon rind**	10 mL
1 cup	**sifted cake flour**	250 mL
½ tsp	**baking powder**	2 mL
	granulated sugar	

- Preheat oven to 375°F (190°C); grease and flour madeleine molds.

- Melt butter; set aside to cool.

- In a large bowl, beat eggs, adding sugar in small amounts, and continue beating for 15 minutes, until mixture is very thick and pale. Add lemon rind.

- Sift flour with baking powder; carefully fold into egg mixture. Add melted butter and mix well.

- Spoon batter into molds, filling them ⅔ full. Bake 10 to 12 minutes, according to size, until edges become golden and cookies spring back when pressed.

- Remove from molds and transfer to wire racks. Sprinkle with granulated sugar and let cool.

F LORENTINES

(2½ dozen)

½ cup	**heavy cream**	125 mL
½ cup	**granulated sugar**	125 mL
¼ cup	**slivered blanched almonds**	50 mL
¼ cup	**finely chopped blanched almonds**	50 mL
1 cup	**finely chopped orange and lemon peel**	250 mL
⅓ cup	**all-purpose flour**	75 mL
6	**squares semi-sweet baking chocolate, melted**	6

- Preheat oven to 350°F (180°C); grease cookie sheets.

- In a bowl, combine cream and sugar; stir in all almonds. In another bowl, combine peel with flour, making sure that peel is well-coated; add to creamed mixture.

- Drop small spoonfuls of batter onto cookie sheet, 3 inches (7.5 cm) apart, baking only 6 at a time. With back of spoon, spread batter as thinly as possible.

- Bake 10 to 12 minutes until edges brown. Let cool about 30 seconds, then carefully remove and place upside-down on another cookie sheet to cool. If florentines stick to cookie sheet and are difficult to remove, return to oven for about 30 seconds to soften. Regrease cookie sheet and repeat with remaining batter.

- When cool, paint bottom of florentines with melted chocolate using a pastry brush. Leave to harden, then store in airtight container.

A MARETTI
(1½ dozen)

2	**egg whites**	2
½ cup	**granulated sugar**	125 mL
1 tbsp	**Amaretto liqueur**	15 mL
¼ tsp	**almond extract**	1 mL
¼ tsp	**baking powder**	1 mL
1 cup	**finely ground almonds**	250 mL

- Preheat oven to 300°F (150°C). Grease and flour a cookie sheet.

- In a large bowl, beat egg whites until fluffy. Gradually add sugar and continue beating until stiff peaks form.

- Fold in liqueur, almond extract, baking powder and ground almonds.

- Spoon about 2 tbsp (30 mL) batter per cookie onto cookie sheet, about 2 inches (5 cm) apart. Bake 25 to 30 minutes until lightly browned. Shut oven off and let amaretti cool inside. Store in an airtight container.

Hazelnut Tuiles

(2 dozen)

1 cup	finely chopped hazelnuts	250 mL
⅔ cup	granulated sugar	150 mL
3 tbsp	all-purpose flour	45 mL
1 tbsp	cornstarch	15 mL
3 tbsp	melted butter	45 mL
1 tbsp	Armagnac liqueur	15 mL
3	large egg whites	3
	pinch of salt	

- Place hazelnuts, sugar, flour, cornstarch and salt in large bowl; mix well. Stir in butter and liqueur.

- Add egg whites, one at a time, mixing between additions. Chill at least 3 hours.

- Preheat oven to 375°F (190°C). Grease and lightly flour cookie sheets.

- Drop small spoonfuls of batter onto cookie sheets, 2 inches (5 cm) apart. Bake 8 minutes or less, depending on size. Do not overcook.

- As soon as they are done, remove carefully with spatula and mold around a rolling pin. When set, transfer to wire racks and let cool.

MANDELBROT

(5 dozen pieces)

3	eggs	3
1 cup	granulated sugar	250 mL
¾ cup	vegetable oil	175 mL
1 tsp	almond extract	5 mL
1 tsp	lemon extract	5 mL
1 tbsp	grated lemon zest	15 mL
3 cups	all-purpose flour	750 mL
2 tsp	baking powder	10 mL
½ cup	shredded coconut	125 mL
½ cup	slivered almonds	125 mL
12	chopped maraschino cherries (optional)	12

- In a large bowl, beat eggs, sugar and oil. Add almond extract, lemon extract, and zest.

- Sift flour with baking powder; stir into beaten egg mixture. Add coconut, almonds and cherries; mix well. Chill for 1 hour.

- Preheat oven to 375°F (190°C). Lightly oil a cookie sheet.

- Divide dough into 4 equal parts. Moisten hands and roll each portion into a thick rope; place on cookie sheet.

- Bake 20 minutes; remove from oven. While still warm, cut into ¾ inch (2 cm) thick slices. Lay flat on cookie sheet and bake 10 minutes until golden. Turn off oven and let cookies cool inside.

SPECULAAS

(3 dozen)

2½ cups	all-purpose flour	625 mL
1 tsp	baking powder	5 mL
1 tsp	cinnamon	5 mL
¼ tsp	ground ginger	1 mL
¼ tsp	ground cardamom	1 mL
¼ tsp	ground nutmeg	1 mL
1 cup	vegetable shortening	250 mL
1 cup	granulated sugar	250 mL
1	egg	1
2 tbsp	milk	30 mL
1 tsp	lemon juice	5 mL
	pinch of white pepper	

- Preheat oven to 350°F (180°C); lightly grease cookie sheets.
- Sift flour with baking powder, cinnamon, ginger, cardamom, nutmeg and pepper.
- In a large bowl, cream shortening with sugar. Add egg, then milk and lemon juice, mixing well after each addition. Stir in spice mixture to make a soft dough.
- Roll dough out ½ inch (1 cm) thick. Shape cookies with a star-shaped cookie cutter. Arrange on cookie sheets and bake 15 to 20 minutes until golden. Transfer cookies to wire racks and let cool.

NOTE: *You can also use a speculaas cookie mold; press dough into mold, then knock it against your work surface to remove from mold. Transfer to cookie sheet and bake.*

Roll dough out ½ inch (1 cm) thick.

Shape cookies with a star-shaped cookie cutter.

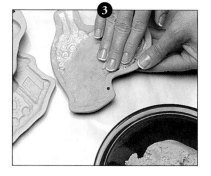

Press dough into speculaas mold.

KICHLACH
(30 pieces)

2	eggs	2
2	egg whites	2
1 cup	vegetable oil	250 mL
6 tbsp	granulated sugar	90 mL
½ tsp	almond extract	2 mL
2 cups	all-purpose flour	500 mL
	granulated sugar	

- Preheat oven to 300°F (150°C). Grease and flour 2 large cookie sheets.

- In a large bowl, beat eggs and egg whites until fluffy. Beating constantly, gradually add oil, sugar and almond extract; continue beating about 4 minutes until batter is thick.

- Fold flour into batter until evenly blended.

- Drop large spoonfuls of batter onto cookie sheet, 2 inches (5 cm) apart. Sprinkle generously with granulated sugar. Bake 25 to 28 minutes, or until golden.

- When done, transfer to wire racks and let cool. Store in an airtight container.

BARS AND SQUARES

Who can say no to delicious bars or squares? Easy and quick to prepare, they will always turn out right if you use the size of pan recommended in the recipe. These wonderful morsels, halfway between cakes and cookies, are just as good for coffee breaks as they are for dessert or a snack.

Whether thick and chewy or thin and crispy, there are so many varieties of bars and squares that young and old alike are sure to ask for more!

NANAIMO SQUARES

(16 squares)

BASE

½ cup	**unsalted butter**	125 mL
¼ cup	**granulated sugar**	50 mL
1	**egg**	1
4 tbsp	**cocoa powder**	60 mL
2 cups	**Graham wafer crumbs**	500 mL
1 cup	**shredded coconut**	250 mL
1 cup	**chopped walnuts**	250 mL

FILLING

¼ cup	**unsalted butter**	50 mL
½ tsp	**vanilla extract**	2 mL
1	**egg**	1
2½ cups	**confectioners' sugar**	625 mL

ICING

4	**squares semi-sweet baking chocolate, chopped**	4
2 tbsp	**unsalted butter**	30 mL
1 tbsp	**water**	15 mL

- In the top of a double-boiler, melt butter with sugar, egg and cocoa powder, stirring constantly until smooth. Stir in Graham wafer crumbs, coconut and walnuts. Spread over the bottom of a 9 inch (23 cm) square cake pan.

- Prepare the filling: cream butter; stir in vanilla, egg and confectioners' sugar. Pour over base in cake pan.

- Prepare the icing: melt chocolate; mix in butter and water. Spread over filling and chill at least 1 hour in the refrigerator. Cut into squares.

DATE AND ORANGE SQUARES

(20 squares)

½ cup	unsalted butter, softened	125 mL
1½ cups	brown sugar	375 mL
1½ cups	all-purpose flour	375 mL
¼ tsp	salt	1 mL
1 tsp	baking powder	5 mL
1¼ cups	oatmeal flakes	300 mL
1 lb	pitted dates	450 g
1	chopped orange	1
1½ cups	water	375 mL

- Preheat oven to 350°F (180°C). Grease a square cake pan.

- In large bowl, cream butter with 1 cup (250 mL) brown sugar. In separate bowl, sift flour with salt and baking powder. Add oatmeal flakes and mix well. Combine dry ingredients with creamed mixture and set aside.

- Place dates, orange, water and remaining brown sugar in saucepan. Bring to a boil and cook until thick. Remove pan from heat and let cool.

- Pack ⅔ of oat mixture into cake pan. Spread date mixture evenly over top. Cover with remaining oat mixture and press lightly.

- Bake 25 minutes. Let cool, then cut into small squares.

CANDIED FRUIT BARS

(2½ dozen)

1½ cups	brown sugar	375 mL
⅓ cup	vegetable oil	75 mL
4	egg whites	4
1¼ cups	all-purpose flour	300 mL
¼ tsp	salt	1 mL
1 tsp	baking soda	5 mL
2½ cups	granola	625 mL
1¼ cups	chopped candied fruit	300 mL
10	chopped candied cherries (optional)	10

- Preheat oven to 350°F (180°C). Grease a 10 x 12 inch (25 x 30 cm) cookie sheet.

- In large bowl, beat brown sugar and oil together about 1 minute. Add egg whites and continue beating 2 to 3 minutes to make a very smooth batter.

- Mix flour with salt and baking soda. Fold into batter along with granola and chopped candied fruit.

- Spread mixture evenly over cookie sheet and bake 20 minutes or until center is cooked. When done, remove from oven and let cool slightly. Cut into small bars and finish cooling on wire rack. Garnish with pieces of candied cherry, if desired.

COCONUT CUBES

(2 dozen)

BASE

¾ cup	honey Graham wafer crumbs	175 mL
3 tbsp	softened vegetable shortening	45 mL

FILLING

2	eggs	2
½ cup	granulated sugar	125 mL
¼ cup	all-purpose flour	50 mL
2¼ cups	shredded coconut	550 mL
1	drop of vanilla extract	1
1 cup	diced pineapple, drained	250 mL
4 tbsp	apricot jam	60 mL

- Preheat oven to 300°F (150°C). Grease an 8 inch (20 cm) square cake pan.

- Prepare the base: mix together Graham wafer crumbs and shortening; set aside.

- Prepare the filling: in a large bowl, whisk eggs with sugar. One after the other, without overmixing, blend in flour, coconut, vanilla and pineapple.

- Press Graham wafer mixture into bottom of cake pan. Pour filling over top. Bake about 45 minutes; let cool. Top with apricot jam and cut into squares.

CHOCOLATE ELVES
(2 dozen)

½ cup	unsalted butter	125 mL
1 cup	brown sugar	250 mL
2	eggs	2
1 cup	all-purpose flour	250 mL
2 tbsp	baking powder	30 mL
¼ tsp	salt	1 mL
¾ cup	walnut pieces	175 mL
1 tsp	vanilla extract	5 mL
	halved walnuts for garnish	

ICING

1 cup	confectioners' sugar	250 mL
1 tbsp	cocoa powder	15 mL
1 tbsp	melted butter	15 mL
2 tbsp	boiling water	30 mL
¼ tsp	vanilla extract	1 mL

- Preheat oven to 325°F (160°C). Grease an 8 inch (20 cm) square cake pan.

- Cream butter with brown sugar. Mix in eggs, one by one. Sift together dry ingredients and add to egg mixture along with walnut pieces and vanilla. Mix well.

- Spread batter in cake pan and bake 30 to 35 minutes. Remove from pan onto a wire rack and let cool.

- Prepare the icing: mix together sugar and cocoa powder. Stir in butter, boiling water and vanilla. Top cake with icing, garnish with halved walnuts and cut into squares.

STRAWBERRY SIDEWALKS

(½ dozen)

1 lb	shortcrust pastry	450 g
1	egg yolk, beaten	1
1	egg white, beaten	1
2 cups	fresh strawberries	500 mL
⅔ cup	granulated sugar	150 mL

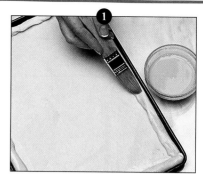

Brush edges with some of egg yolk, ¾ inch (2 cm) on every side, then fold over to make a ½ inch (1 cm) crust.

- Preheat oven to 375°F (190°C). Grease a cookie sheet.

- Roll ⅔ of pastry into a 9 x 11 inch (23 x 28 cm) rectangle and place on cookie sheet. Brush edges with some of egg yolk, ¾ inch (2 cm) on every side, then fold over to make a ½ inch (1 cm) crust. Brush pastry with egg white and prick with a fork.

- Bake 8 minutes. Remove from oven and reduce oven temperature to 350°F (180°C).

- Wash, hull and slice strawberries. Sprinkle with sugar and arrange over pastry on cookie sheet. Roll out remaining pastry and cut into ¼ inch (0.5 cm) wide strips. Arrange over strawberries in a crisscross pattern. Brush ends with remaining egg yolk to secure them to the crust.

- Bake 20 to 25 minutes. Cut into squares. Serve hot or cold.

Brush pastry with egg white and prick with a fork.

VARIATION: Apple Sidewalks. Substitute strawberries with 2 cups (500 mL) peeled and sliced apples.

Distribute strawberries over pastry.

Roll out remaining pastry and cut into ¼ inch (0.5 cm) wide strips. Arrange strips over strawberries in a crisscross pattern.

MERINGUE DATE SQUARES

(8 bites)

1½ cups	pitted dates	375 mL
¾ cup	coffee or water	175 mL
⅓ cup	unsalted butter	75 mL
½ cup	granulated sugar	125 mL
2	egg yolks	2
1 tsp	almond extract	5 mL
1 tbsp	almond liqueur	15 mL
1½ cups	all-purpose flour	375 mL
1 tsp	baking powder	5 mL
¼ tsp	salt	1 mL
½ cup	milk	125 mL
2	egg whites	2
¾ cup	packed brown sugar	175 mL
½ cup	blanched slivered almonds	125 mL

- Preheat oven to 350°F (180°C). Grease and flour a 6 x 10 inch (15 x 25 cm) cake pan; line with ovenproof waxed paper.

- In a saucepan over medium heat, cook dates with coffee 10 minutes. Cover with plastic wrap and set aside.

- In a large bowl, cream butter with sugar. Mix in egg yolks, almond extract and liqueur. Sift together flour, baking powder and salt; gradually stir into almond mixture, alternating with milk. Set batter aside.

- Beat egg whites until stiff peaks form. Gradually mix in brown sugar to make a firm meringue.

- Spread batter in cake pan. Cover with date mixture and top with meringue. Sprinkle with slivered almonds and bake 30 minutes. When done, cut into squares.

MARBLED TOFFEE SQUARES

(1 dozen)

1 cup	unsalted butter, softened	250 mL
1¼ cups	brown sugar	300 mL
1	egg	1
2¼ cups	all-purpose flour	550 mL
¼ tsp	salt	1 mL
1 cup	chopped pecans	250 mL
½ cup	chocolate chips	125 mL
2	squares white baking chocolate	2
2	squares semi-sweet baking chocolate	2

- Preheat oven to 350°F (180°C). Lightly grease and flour a cake pan.

- Cream butter in large bowl. Add brown sugar and continue beating until light and fluffy. Beat in egg.

- Sift flour with salt and stir into batter. Add pecans and chocolate chips; mix well.

- Pour batter into cake pan and bake 25 minutes. Remove from oven.

- Melt white chocolate and semi-sweet chocolate separately. Drop large spoonfuls of each onto cake and marble with a knife. Cut into small squares while still warm and let cool. Transfer to wire rack and cool completely.

STRAWBERRY NUT BARS
(3 dozen)

¾ cup	vegetable shortening	175 mL
⅓ cup	unsalted butter	75 mL
1⅓ cups	granulated sugar	325 mL
3	eggs, beaten	3
2 tsp	grated orange zest	10 mL
3 cups	all-purpose flour	750 mL
¾ tsp	baking soda	4 mL
1½ cups	strawberry jam	375 mL
¾ cup	chopped walnuts	175 mL

- Preheat oven to 375°F (190°C).

- In a bowl, cream together shortening, butter and sugar. Add eggs and orange zest; mix well. Sift together flour and baking soda and stir into batter.

- Pour batter into an 8 x 12 inch (20 x 30 cm) cake pan. Bake about 20 minutes, or until a toothpick inserted into center comes out clean. Top with strawberry jam and let cool. Sprinkle with walnuts and cut into 1 x 3 inch (2.5 x 8 cm) bars.

PEANUT AND RAISIN SQUARES
(2 dozen)

1½ cups	peanuts	375 mL
1½ cups	oatmeal flakes	375 mL
3 cups	raisins	750 mL
¾ cup	peanut butter	175 mL
	toasted shredded coconut (optional)	

- Grind peanuts in a food processor. Add oatmeal flakes, raisins and peanut butter; process into a batter.

- Pour batter into a 13 x 9 inch (33 x 23 cm) cake pan. Sprinkle with coconut, if desired. Cover and chill 1 hour in the refrigerator. Cut into 2 inch (5 cm) squares.

CHOCOLATE OATMEAL TRIANGLES
(18 pieces)

½ cup	milk	125 mL
½ cup	unsalted butter	125 mL
⅓ cup	cocoa powder	75 mL
2 cups	granulated sugar	500 mL
3 cups	oatmeal flakes	750 mL
1½ cups	shredded coconut	375 mL

- In a saucepan, whisk together milk, butter, cocoa and sugar. Bring to a boil, remove from heat and fold in oats and coconut.

- Grease a 9 inch (23 cm) square cake pan; pour batter into pan. Let cool before cutting into triangles or squares. Cover and keep refrigerated.

PEANUT BUTTER GRANOLA BARS
(2 dozen)

⅓ cup	melted unsalted butter	75 mL
½ cup	packed brown sugar	125 mL
⅓ cup	peanut butter	75 mL
1	egg, beaten	1
½ tsp	vanilla extract	2 mL
½ cup	coconut flakes	125 mL
4 cups	whole wheat, bran, fruit and fiber cereal	1 L
	fresh strawberries, halved	

- Preheat oven to 300°F (150°C). Grease a cake pan.

- In a large bowl, mix together butter, brown sugar, peanut butter, egg and vanilla. Gently fold in coconut and cereal.

- Pour batter into cake pan and press lightly. Bake 30 minutes. Remove from oven and cut into bars. Let cool and remove from cake pan. Garnish with fresh strawberries.

ℬANANA BRAN SQUARES
(6 dozen)

1 cup	all-purpose flour	250 mL
1 cup	wheat bran	250 mL
¼ cup	granulated sugar	50 mL
1 ½ tsp	baking powder	7 mL
½ tsp	baking soda	2 mL
½ tsp	salt	2 mL
¼ cup	margarine	50 mL
½ cup	yogurt	125 mL
1 cup	mashed banana	250 mL
¼ cup	milk	50 mL
	hazelnut spread	
	banana slices	

• Preheat oven to 350°F (180°C). Grease a 9 inch (23 cm) square cake pan.

• In a large bowl, mix together dry ingredients. Stir in margarine to make a lumpy mixture. In another bowl, combine yogurt, mashed banana and milk. Blend into first mixture.

• Spread batter into cake pan. Bake about 40 minutes. Let cool slightly, then top with hazelnut spread. Garnish with slices of banana and cut into squares.

CRANBERRY OAT SQUARES

(9 squares)

12 oz	cranberries	340 g
1 cup	granulated sugar	250 mL
½ cup	raisins	125 mL
1 tbsp	cornstarch	15 mL
2 tbsp	cold water	30 mL
1 cup	all-purpose flour	250 mL
1½ tsp	baking soda	7 mL
1 cup	cold unsalted butter	250 mL
1 cup	brown sugar	250 mL
2 cups	oatmeal flakes	500 mL
	pinch of salt	

- Preheat oven to 350°F (180°C).

- In a saucepan, cook cranberries with granulated sugar until soft, about 5 minutes. Purée with a potato masher and cook 10 to 15 minutes. Add raisins and continue cooking 2 minutes. Dissolve cornstarch in cold water and add to purée; cook until mixture thickens. Remove from heat and cover with plastic wrap; let cool.

- Meanwhile, sift together flour, baking soda and salt. Cut butter into dry ingredients and mix to make a lumpy batter. Mix in brown sugar and oatmeal flakes.

- Spread half of batter into a 9 inch (23 cm) square cake pan. Cover evenly with cranberry purée, and then with remaining oat batter.

- Bake 30 minutes and let cool slightly before cutting into squares.

MACADAMIA NUT AND ALMOND BROWNIES

(16 slices)

1½ cups	**semi-sweet chocolate chips**	375 mL
1 cup	**unsalted butter**	250 mL
1¾ cups	**brown sugar**	425 mL
4	**large eggs**	4
1 tsp	**vanilla extract**	5 mL
1¾ cups	**cake flour**	425 mL
¼ tsp	**salt**	1 mL
1 cup	**macadamia nuts**	250 mL
1 cup	**slivered almonds**	250 mL

- Preheat oven to 375°F (190°C). Grease and flour two 9 inch (23 cm) round baking pans.

- Melt chocolate chips in top of double-boiler over low heat.

- In large bowl, beat butter and brown sugar together until fluffy. Stir in melted chocolate and mix well. Beat in eggs and vanilla.

- Sift flour with salt and stir into batter. Mix in macadamia nuts and almonds.

- Divide batter evenly between pans, smoothing tops with spatula. Bake 30 to 40 minutes or until toothpick inserted into center comes out clean.

- When done, remove from oven and let cool. Sprinkle with confectioners' sugar and serve.

Stir melted chocolate into butter mixture.

Stir in sifted flour and salt.

Mix in macadamia nuts and almonds.

Divide batter evenly between pans.

ℬUTTERSCOTCH BROWNIES

(1 dozen)

1 cup	unsalted butter, softened	250 mL
1¾ cups	brown sugar	425 mL
2	large eggs	2
1 tsp	vanilla extract	5 mL
2¼ cups	all-purpose flour	550 mL
1¼ cups	butterscotch chips	300 mL
1	square semi-sweet chocolate, melted	1

• Preheat oven to 350°F (180°C). Butter and lightly flour a 2 inch (5 cm) deep rectangular baking pan.

• In large bowl, beat butter with brown sugar until creamy. Beat in eggs and vanilla; continue beating until fluffy.

• Sift flour and fold into batter. Fold in butterscotch chips.

• Using spatula, scrape batter into baking pan and smooth top evenly. Bake 25 to 30 minutes in oven or until toothpick inserted in center comes out clean.

• When done, remove from oven and let cool. Cut into small bars and drizzle with melted chocolate.

MUFFINS

The wonderful textures and flavors of muffins make them one of the simple pleasures in life. Prepared in no time, they are delicious hot or cold and lend themselves well to many occasions. A lot of people like them for breakfast, while others enjoy them as a snack.

If there's a secret to making muffins, it's that you mustn't overmix the ingredients. This way they'll come out light and fluffy and melt in your mouth. These little cakes are so delicious that once you've had one, it's hard to resist another!

ℬLUEBERRY MUFFINS

(1 dozen)

2 cups	all-purpose flour	500 mL
¾ cup	granulated sugar	175 mL
4 tsp	baking powder	20 mL
½ tsp	salt	2 mL
1	egg	1
¾ cup	milk	175 mL
⅓ cup	vegetable oil	75 mL
1 cup	fresh blueberries	250 mL

- Preheat oven to 350°F (180°C). Grease a muffin tin.

- Sift dry ingredients together into a large bowl. In another bowl, beat egg with milk, then add oil. Fold into dry ingredients, mixing lightly, until the batter comes away from the sides of the bowl. Fold in blueberries.

- Spoon batter into muffin tin, filling cups about ¾ full. Bake 18 to 20 minutes, or until a toothpick inserted into center comes out clean. When done, remove muffins immediately from tin.

Ⓜ︎APLE WALNUT AND BANANA MUFFINS

(1 dozen)

2 cups	whole wheat flour	500 mL
4 tsp	baking powder	20 mL
¾ cups	granulated maple sugar	175 mL
½ cup	vegetable oil	125 mL
2	eggs, beaten	2
2	bananas, mashed	2
1 cup	milk	250 mL
¾ cup	walnut pieces	175 mL
	pinch of salt	

- Preheat oven to 350°F (180°C). Grease a muffin tin.

- In a large bowl, combine flour, baking powder, salt, maple sugar and oil. With a wooden spoon, mix in eggs, bananas, milk and nuts.

- Spoon batter into muffin tin, filling cups about ¾ full. Bake about 15 minutes, or until a toothpick inserted into center comes out clean.

ORANGE DATE MUFFINS

(1 dozen)

1 cup	pitted dates	250 mL
1	unpeeled orange	1
½ cup	all-purpose flour	125 mL
⅓ cup	unsalted butter	75 mL
¾ cup	granulated sugar	175 mL
2	eggs	2
½ cup	orange juice	125 mL
¾ cup	whole wheat flour	175 mL
1 cup	all-purpose flour	250 mL
2 tsp	baking powder	10 mL
¾ tsp	baking soda	4 mL
½ tsp	salt	2 mL

- Preheat oven to 400°F (200°C). Line muffin tin with paper cups.

- Coarsely chop dates and orange, and combine with ½ cup (125 mL) all-purpose flour.

- In a large bowl, gently mix together butter and sugar until smooth but not fluffy. Stirring constantly, add eggs, one by one, and then orange juice. Blend in remaining dry ingredients and date mixture.

- Spoon batter into muffin tin, filling cups about ¾ full. Bake 15 minutes, or until a toothpick inserted in center comes out clean. Remove muffins from tin and serve hot or cold.

Coarsely chop dates and orange, and combine with ½ cup (125 mL) all-purpose flour.

Add eggs, one by one, to butter mixture.

Blend in remaining dry ingredients and date mixture.

CRANBERRY POPPY SEED MUFFINS

(1 dozen)

2½ cups	cake flour	625 mL
1 tsp	salt	5 mL
2 tsp	baking powder	10 mL
1 tsp	baking soda	5 mL
⅓ cup	granulated sugar	75 mL
¾ cup	milk	175 mL
2	small eggs, lightly beaten	2
4 tbsp	melted unsalted butter	60 mL
1¼ cups	dried cranberries	300 mL
3 tbsp	poppy seeds	45 mL

- Preheat oven to 400°F (200°C). Grease a muffin tin.
- Sift all dry ingredients together.
- In a separate bowl, whisk milk with eggs and melted butter. Using wooden spoon, fold in dry ingredients, then cranberries and poppy seeds.
- Spoon batter into muffin tin, filling cups about ¾ full. Bake 20 to 25 minutes or until tops spring back when lightly pressed.
- When done, remove from oven and turn out onto wire rack to cool.

APPLE AND WHEAT GERM MUFFINS

(1 dozen)

1 ¼ cups	all-purpose flour	300 mL
¾ cup	brown sugar	175 mL
1 tbsp	baking powder	15 mL
½ tsp	salt	2 mL
1 tsp	cinnamon	5 mL
½ tsp	ground nutmeg	2 mL
¾ cup	wheat germ	175 mL
2	apples, peeled and grated	2
½ cup	raisins	125 mL
2	eggs	2
½ cup	milk	125 mL
3 tbsp	sunflower oil	45 mL
1	batch icing (see recipe page 244)	1

- Preheat oven to 375°F (190°C). Grease a muffin tin.

- In a large bowl, combine dry ingredients. Add wheat germ, grated apple and raisins; mix well.

- In a separate bowl, beat eggs, then beat in milk and oil. Stir into apple mixture.

- Spoon batter into muffin tin, filling cups about ⅔ full. Bake 20 to 30 minutes, or until a toothpick inserted into center comes out clean.

- Let cool slightly before removing from tin. Top with icing.

𝒞HEDDAR MUFFINS
(1 dozen)

2 cups	whole wheat flour	500 mL
2 tsp	baking powder	10 mL
½ tsp	salt	2 mL
1 cup	grated old cheddar cheese	250 mL
1 cup	milk	250 mL
⅓ cup	honey	75 mL
1	egg	1
⅓ cup	melted unsalted butter	75 mL

𝓬

- Preheat oven to 400°F (200°C). Grease a muffin tin.

- In a large bowl, mix together flour, baking powder, salt and cheddar cheese. In another bowl, combine milk, honey, egg and butter. Add, all at once, to dry ingredients; fold in without overmixing.

- Spoon batter into muffin tin, filling cups about ¾ full. Bake about 20 minutes, or until toothpick inserted into center comes out clean.

𝒩OTE: *these muffins will keep up to 6 months in the freezer. To defrost, leave them in the refrigerator for 24 hours.*

RAISIN BRAN MUFFINS
(1 dozen)

½ cup	whole wheat flour	125 mL
⅔ cup	all-purpose flour	150 mL
1 cup	brown sugar	250 mL
1 tbsp	baking powder	15 mL
½ tsp	baking soda	2 mL
½ tsp	ground nutmeg	2 mL
½ tsp	salt	2 mL
¾ cup	bran	175 mL
1	large egg	1
¾ cup	buttermilk	175 mL
½ cup	sunflower oil	125 mL
½ cup	raisins, coated in flour	125 mL

- Preheat oven to 425°F (220°C). Grease muffin tin or line with paper cups.

- In a large bowl, combine both flours, brown sugar, baking powder, baking soda, nutmeg and salt. Add bran and mix well.

- In a separate bowl, beat egg. Whisk in buttermilk and oil.

- Blend egg mixture into dry ingredients without over-mixing. Fold in raisins. Spoon batter into muffin tin, filling cups about ¾ full. Bake 18 to 20 minutes.

- Remove from oven and let cool several minutes before turning out onto wire racks.

PECAN AND MAPLE MUFFINS

(1 dozen)

2 cups	whole wheat flour	500 mL
½ tsp	salt	2 mL
1 tbsp	baking powder	15 mL
½ cup	maple syrup	125 mL
4 tbsp	vegetable oil	60 mL
2	eggs, beaten	2
4 tbsp	milk	60 mL
½ cup	pecan pieces	125 mL
⅜ cup	granulated maple sugar	100 mL
¼ cup	oatmeal flakes	50 mL
2 tbsp	melted unsalted butter	30 mL

- Preheat oven to 375°F (190°C). Grease and flour a muffin tin.

- Combine whole wheat flour, salt and baking powder. In a large bowl, mix together maple syrup, oil, eggs and milk. Gradually mix in dry ingredients and fold in pecans.

- Spoon batter into muffin tin, filling cups about ¾ full.

- Combine maple sugar, oatmeal and melted butter; sprinkle over muffins. Bake about 20 minutes, or until toothpick inserted into center comes out clean. Remove muffins from tin.

Gradually mix dry ingredients into maple syrup mixture.

Spoon batter into muffin tin.

Combine maple sugar, oatmeal and melted butter; sprinkle over muffins.

CARROT MUFFINS
(1 dozen)

½ cup	granulated sugar	125 mL
⅔ cup	honey	150 mL
½ cup	vegetable oil	125 mL
3	eggs	3
1⅔ cups	all-purpose flour	400 mL
2 tsp	cinnamon	10 mL
¾ tsp	baking soda	4 mL
1 tbsp	baking powder	15 mL
2 cups	grated carrot	500 mL
½ cup	raisins	125 mL
½ cup	chopped walnuts	125 mL
	pinch of ground clove	

ICING

½ cup	unsalted butter	125 mL
½ cup	cream cheese	125 mL
1 cup	confectioners' sugar	250 mL
1 tbsp	lemon zest	15 mL
1 tsp	lemon juice	5 mL

- Preheat oven to 400°F (200°C). Line muffin tin with paper cups.

- In a large bowl, combine sugar, honey and oil, mixing until smooth. Stirring constantly, add eggs, one by one.

- Sift together flour, cinnamon, clove, baking soda and baking powder. Fold these dry ingredients into egg mixture, then fold in carrot, raisins and walnuts.

- Spoon batter into muffin tin, filling cups about ¾ full. Bake 15 minutes, or until toothpick inserted into center comes out clean. Remove muffins from tin and serve hot, or let cool and decorate with icing.

- To prepare icing, cream together butter and cream cheese. Add sugar and mix well. Blend in lemon zest and juice.

PUMPKIN MUFFINS
(1 dozen)

¾ cup	honey	175 mL
½ cup	vegetable oil	125 mL
1 cup	cold pumpkin purée*	250 mL
2	eggs	2
1 tsp	almond extract	5 mL
1½ cups	whole wheat flour	375 mL
1 tsp	baking powder	5 mL
½ tsp	baking soda	2 mL
½ tsp	salt	2 mL
2 tsp	all-purpose flour	10 mL
⅓ cup	raisins	75 mL
¼ cup	walnuts	50 mL

- Preheat oven to 350°F (180°C). Grease muffin tin or line with paper cups.

- In a large bowl, combine honey, oil, pumpkin purée, eggs and almond extract. Sift together whole wheat flour, baking powder, baking soda and salt; add to pumpkin batter.

- Lightly flour raisins and walnuts and fold into batter. Spoon batter into muffin tin, filling cups about ¾ full. Bake 25 to 30 minutes, or until toothpick inserted into center comes out clean.

* To make pumpkin purée, cut a pumpkin in half, remove the seeds, and bake 30 minutes at 350°F (180°C). Spoon out flesh and purée in a food processor. Let cool.

246

WHOLE WHEAT CAROB CHIP MUFFINS
(1 dozen)

3 cups	whole wheat flour	750 mL
½ cup	cake flour	125 mL
2 tbsp	baking powder	30 mL
1 cup	brown sugar	250 mL
2	eggs, beaten	2
1 cup	milk	250 mL
¾ cup	vegetable oil	175 mL
1 tsp	vanilla extract	5 mL
½ cup	carob chips*	125 mL

- Preheat oven to 400°F (200°C). Grease a muffin tin.

- In a bowl, mix together dry ingredients. Add eggs, then remaining ingredients, stirring vigorously with wooden spoon.

- Spoon batter into muffin tin, filling cups about ¾ full. Bake 15 minutes, or until muffins are golden and a toothpick inserted into center comes out clean.

* Carob chips can be found at natural food stores.

GINGER AND RASPBERRY MUFFINS

(1 dozen)

1½ cups	cake flour	375 mL
1 tsp	salt	5 mL
1 cup	oat flour	250 mL
2 tsp	baking powder	10 mL
1 tsp	baking soda	5 mL
⅓ cup	brown sugar	75 mL
¾ cup	milk	175 mL
2	small eggs, lightly beaten	2
4 tbsp	melted butter	60 mL
¼ cup	finely chopped candied ginger	50 mL
¾ cup	fresh raspberries	175 mL
¼ cup	honey	50 mL

- Preheat oven to 400°F (200°C). Grease a muffin tin.
- Sift all dry ingredients together. In separate bowl, whisk milk with eggs and melted butter. Using wooden spoon, fold in dry ingredients and ginger.
- Combine raspberries and honey; set aside.
- Spoon batter into muffin tin, filling cups about ⅓ full. Place 4 or 5 raspberries in the center of each muffin and cover with remaining batter. Bake 20 to 25 minutes or until tops spring back when lightly pressed.
- When done, remove from oven and turn out onto wire racks to cool.

Spoon batter into muffin tin, filling cups about ⅓ full.

Place 4 or 5 raspberries in the center of each muffin.

Cover with remaining batter.

CHUNKY CHOCOLATE CHIP MUFFINS
(1 dozen)

2½ cups	cake flour	625 mL
1 tsp	salt	5 mL
2 tsp	baking powder	10 mL
1 tsp	baking soda	5 mL
3 tbsp	granulated sugar	45 mL
¾ cup	milk	175 mL
2	small eggs, lightly beaten	2
4 tbsp	melted unsalted butter	60 mL
3	squares semi-sweet baking chocolate, in chunks	3
½ cup	semi-sweet chocolate chips	125 mL

- Preheat oven to 400°F (200°C). Grease a muffin tin.

- Sift all dry ingredients together; set aside.

- In a large bowl, whisk milk with eggs and melted butter. Using wooden spoon, fold in dry ingredients, then chocolate chunks and chips.

- Spoon batter into muffin tin, filling cups about ¾ full. Bake 20 minutes or until tops spring back when lightly pressed.

- When done, remove from oven and transfer to wire rack to cool.

*O*ATMEAL FIG MUFFINS

(1 dozen)

1 cup	oatmeal flakes	250 mL
1½ cups	all-purpose flour	375 mL
½ tsp	salt	2 mL
4 tsp	baking powder	20 mL
1 tsp	baking soda	5 mL
¾ cup	brown sugar	175 mL
¾ cup	milk	175 mL
1	egg, lightly beaten	1
⅓ cup	sunflower oil	75 mL
1 cup	chopped dried figs	250 mL

ᦞ

- Preheat oven to 400°F (200°C). Grease a muffin tin.
- Sift all dry ingredients together.
- In separate bowl, whisk milk with egg and sunflower oil. Using wooden spoon, fold in dry ingredients and figs.
- Spoon batter into muffin tin, filling cups about ¾ full. Bake 20 minutes or until tops spring back when lightly pressed.
- When done, remove from oven and turn out onto wire rack to cool, or serve warm with butter and jam.

RAISIN CORN MUFFINS

(1 dozen)

2	eggs	2
¾ cup	granulated sugar	175 mL
¾ cup	corn flour	175 mL
1¼ cups	cake flour	300 mL
2 tsp	baking powder	10 mL
¾ cup	milk	175 mL
½ cup	vegetable oil	125 mL
⅓ cup	golden raisins	75 mL
	pinch of salt	

- Preheat oven to 350°F (180°C). Grease a muffin tin.
- In a large bowl, beat eggs and sugar until fluffy. In another bowl, sift together corn flour, cake flour, baking powder and salt. In a small bowl combine milk and oil.
- Gradually add dry ingredients to egg mixture, alternating with milk and oil. Fold in raisins.
- Spoon batter into muffin tin, filling cups about ¾ full. Bake 20 minutes, or until a toothpick inserted into center comes out clean.

HONEY BUCKWHEAT MUFFINS

(1 dozen)

1 cup	cake flour	250 mL
1 cup	buckwheat flour	250 mL
4 tsp	baking powder	20 mL
2	eggs, beaten	2
½ cup	buckwheat honey*	125 mL
¾ cup	milk	175 mL
½ cup	vegetable oil	125 mL
	pinch of salt	

- Preheat oven to 350°F (180°C). Grease a muffin tin.
- In a large bowl, mix together dry ingredients. Add eggs and remaining ingredients; mix with a wooden spoon.
- Spoon batter into muffin tin, filling cups about ¾ full. Bake 15 minutes, or until toothpick inserted into center comes out clean.

* Buckwheat honey can be found in natural food stores and fine supermarkets.

Index